Rebecca

starring

CHARLES DANCE,
DIANA RIGG,
EMILIA FOX
AND FAYE DUNAWAY

The official story behind ITV's making of Daphne du Maurier's classic tale of love and jealousy

GEOFF TIBBALLS

CHAMELEON

First published in Great Britain in 1996 by
Chameleon Books
106 Great Russell Street
London WC1B 3LJ

The right of Geoff Tibballs to be identified as the author of this work has been
asserted by him in accordance with the Copyright, Design and Patents Act 1988.

ISBN 0 233 99054 2

CIP data for this title is available from the British Library.

Printed in Great Britain by Caledonian International, Glasgow.

Page 1:
Charles Dance as Mr
Maxim de Winter and
Emilia Fox as the
young girl.

Page 2:
Emilia Fox.

Contents

Acknowledgements

The author would like to thank the following for their co-operation in the preparation of this book: cast members Charles Dance, Diana Rigg, Emilia Fox, Faye Dunaway, Jonathan Cake, Geraldine James and Lucy Cohu; Christian Browning, Daphne du Maurier's son and the literary executor of her estate; writer Arthur Hopcraft; from the production team Hilary Heath, Jim O'Brien, Robin Lowe, Caroline Amies, Doreen Jones, Mark Mostyn, Liz Waller, Aileen Seaton, Frank Walsh, Joss Williams and Sÿa Russell; Sian Facer, Peter Mares, Nick Lockett and Barry Ledingham from Carlton UK Television; BBC Written Archives at Caversham; and Deborah Waight at Chameleon Books. Thanks also to Gollancz and Curtis Brown for permission to quote from *Rebecca* and *The Rebecca Notebooks*.

Opposite:
Charles Dance.

Introduction

Last night I dreamt I went to Manderley again. It seemed to me I stood by the iron gate leading to the drive, and for a while I could not enter for the way was barred to me. There was a padlock and a chain upon the gate. I called in my dream to the lodge-keeper, and had no answer, and peering closer through the rusted spokes of the gate I saw that the lodge was uninhabited.

These are the famous opening lines of *Rebecca*, Daphne du Maurier's dark tale of love, jealousy and insecurity set against the brooding backdrop of a rambling Cornish country house. Published in 1938, *Rebecca* has been hailed as the prototype for the modern Gothic novel, a work on a par with Charlotte Brontë's classic *Jane Eyre*. It has spawned a successful film, a stage play, television adaptations, radio productions, even an opera, and is still a bestseller throughout the world, just as it was almost sixty years ago. *Rebecca* also established Daphne du Maurier as one of the most accomplished novelists of the twentieth century and ensured that her name, along with that of her beloved Cornwall, would be immortalised in English literature long after her death.

The magic of *Rebecca* has never diminished and now a new generation can enjoy this most enduring of stories in a lavish two-part television production from Portman Productions, co-produced with Carlton UK Television and WGBH Boston, and made in association with Tele-münchen of Germany. As befits an international production, there is a truly international cast, headed by Charles Dance as Maxim de Winter, Diana Rigg as Mrs Danvers, Faye Dunaway as Mrs Van Hopper and introducing Emilia Fox as the second Mrs de Winter.

This book traces the story behind the four million pound production, and includes the search for Manderley, the quest for authentic period costumes and interviews with the stars. The adaptation of *Rebecca* by Arthur Hopcraft, the writer who did such a wonderful job on John le Carré's *Tinker, Tailor, Soldier, Spy*, retells the novel for a 1990's audience whilst retaining the essential spirit of the original. As the director Jim O'Brien concludes: 'For me, it was the opportunity to tell an extremely powerful and well-loved story in a fresh way, with outstanding actors.'

CHAPTER ONE

The World of Daphne du Maurier

Daphne du Maurier was born in London on 13 May 1907, to a family rich in both financial and artistic terms. The du Mauriers were descended from French master craftsmen glass-blowers who had managed to flee the Revolution. Daphne's grandfather, George du Maurier (1834-1896), was renowned for the satirical cartoons he drew for *Punch* magazine and for his novels such as *Peter Ibbetson* and *Trilby*. Her father Gerald – suave, sophisticated and a renowned ladies' man (Daphne described him as having a 'wandering eye') – was one of the most celebrated actor-managers of his day, a veritable matinée idol. He was involved in the running of Wyndham's Theatre on Charing Cross Road, a venue often referred to as 'Gerald's theatre'. Her mother, Muriel Beaumont, was also an actress before eventually relinquishing her career to raise a family. In the circumstances, it was scarcely surprising that all three du Maurier daughters should soon display a leaning towards the arts.

Daphne was the middle sister, between Angela (born in 1904) and Jeanne (born in 1911). The du Maurier family home was suitably impressive, a large house at 24 Cumberland Terrace near Regents Park, where the girls were protected from the squalors of Edwardian London. Theirs was certainly a privileged upbringing, with frequent holidays to Cannes and Monte Carlo. Money was no object and Gerald du Maurier enjoyed spending it. A constant stream of actors and sundry theatrical folk visited the house. While Jeanne developed a talent for painting and Angela followed in her father's footsteps by taking to the stage, Daphne, described as the prettiest of the three, buried herself in books. She was less confident than her sisters and often retreated into fiction as an escape from the rounds of visitors. She preferred to live away from the spotlight, a trait which would manifest itself again in the later years of her life.

In 1916, the family moved even further upmarket, to Cannon Hall, a splendid Hampstead mansion built by George III for his physician. It was there that, encouraged by her governess, Miss Waddell, the thirteen-year-old Daphne made her first real foray into writing, inventing characters to people a series of short stories. Over the next few years, she continued to read and write, hoping one day to be as good as Katherine Mansfield. Eventually Daphne showed some of her compositions to her father, who was so impressed that he asked his secretary to type them up. He in turn showed them to her uncle, Comyns Beaumont, editor of *The Bystander* magazine, who offered to publish one, *And Now God the Father*, for a fee of ten guineas provided that she was willing to cut it down to size. At first she flatly refused to do so, but ultimately gave in and the story was duly published, along with one of her poems.

Daphne was extremely close to her father, but her relationship with her mother was somewhat more distant, at least until after Gerald du Maurier's death. Although Gerald lived a typically colourful theatrical life he was a strict parent and did not encourage his daughters to have boyfriends. Angela and Jeanne never married; it was said that they became afraid of men. Daphne meanwhile embarked on three formative relationships. The first was with a cousin, Geoffrey Millar, a married man and twenty-two years her senior. It began when she was just fourteen but never progressed beyond the platonic. She later remarked that he was more like a brother to her. The second relationship, with young film director Carol Reed, was more serious and lasted for some years but was destined not to end in marriage. The third was with Mlle Fernande Yvon, *directrice* of the Paris finishing school Daphne attended in 1924. Daphne developed a crush on Mlle Yvon, searching, it is thought, for the mother/daughter relationship which was missing from her life. The relationship was entirely innocent but the intense friendship between the two women continued until Mlle Yvon's untimely death from leukaemia.

> Theirs was certainly a privileged upbringing, with frequent holidays to Cannes and Monte Carlo. Money was no object ...

But Daphne was to find an even greater love – Cornwall. She had always enjoyed holidays in the country, seeing them as a welcome escape from the hectic social whirl of the London theatre crowd. Boosted by the tremendous financial success of Gerald du Maurier's latest production, *The Ringer* (written by Edgar Wallace), the family began looking for a summer home and, in September 1926, Muriel took the three girls down to Looe. They were distinctly unimpressed but decided to hire a car and journey on to Fowey. En route, they stopped for lunch at the Ferry Inn at Bodinnick, across the Fowey River from Fowey itself. They noticed a For Sale sign on a gate near the ferry and further inspection revealed a rambling three-storey house called Swiss Cottage. Daphne in particular was captivated by the location. Straight after lunch, she went back to the old house and gazed out over the estuary and Fowey harbour, breathing in the solitude and freedom which were so absent in London. The only thing the family objected to was the house's name – Swiss Cottage held too many memories of London's bustling Finchley Road – and so, on completing the purchase, they re-christened it Ferryside.

The acquisition of Ferryside was a turning point in Daphne du Maurier's life. At last she had found a place where she could be at peace with the world. Paris and London retreated into insignificance as Cornwall became her spiritual home and inspired her literary endeavours. Many years later, she wrote 'When the hired car swept around the curve of the hill, the full expanse of Fowey harbour was beneath us. The whole vista was like a gateway to another world. Here, I thought, was the freedom I had sought, and not yet found. Here was the freedom and solace to walk, sail, go fishing, and even perhaps to write.'

Ironically, Gerald du Maurier was never really comfortable at Ferryside. A man who was easily bored, he missed the bright lights of London and his mood was not improved by the torrential rain which greeted his first visit to Fowey. Knowing that his family loved the place, he tolerated it for short periods but could never wait to get back to the city.

Daphne, on the other hand, eagerly explored the surrounding area, making a mental note of locations and of the characters she met on the way. On one afternoon walk, she cut through woods to the head of Pont Creek, an estuary which

Maxim de Winter (Charles Dance) with the girl (Emilia Fox) who is to become the second Mrs de Winter.

Maxim receives Mrs Van Hopper's invitation to join her and her companion at their table.

separates the villages of Bodinnick and Polruan. There she came upon the wreck of an old schooner, the *Jane Slade*, which lay abandoned on the mud flats. Daphne was intrigued by the vessel and set about probing into its history. She discovered that the Slade family had owned a boat-building yard in Polruan and when she was given a bundle of old letters which had belonged to the Slades, her imagination ran riot. Here she could see the basis for her first novel.

At Ferryside in October 1929, she set to work on the manuscript. Her short story *And Now God the Father* had just been published in *The Bystander* and she had excitedly bought a copy of the magazine in Fowey to see her name in print. Impressed by her work, her uncle had introduced her to the literary agency Curtis Brown through whom she met the future publisher Michael Joseph. It was Joseph who encouraged her with the novel, which she decided would be called *The Loving Spirit* after a poem by Emily Brontë. For the purposes of the book, the Slade family became the Coombes and Polruan became the fictional fishing village of Plyn. She finished the 200,000 words, all written by hand, in just over three months and *The Loving Spirit* was published in 1931, both in Britain and the United States, for an advance fee of sixty-seven pounds. There seems little doubt that the du Maurier name helped smooth her way through the minefield of publishing and assisted Daphne, as a new author, in having her work accepted. Indeed, the *Times* review of *The Loving Spirit* concluded: 'Miss du Maurier's power of depicting the life of the little Cornish port and her sympathetic touch upon the emotional stops give promise that with the gaining of firmer outline and greater

Opposite:
Mrs Van Hopper (Faye Dunaway) and the girl (Emilia Fox) enjoy Maxim's company.

experience, she will tread very worthily in her grandfather's footsteps.'

To Daphne's amazement *The Loving Spirit* became an immediate bestseller. Among those who read the book avidly was Frederick Browning, an officer in the Grenadiers who was nicknamed 'Boy' on account of his youthful features, although Daphne came to know him as 'Tommy'. He was so captivated by the novel that he decided to sail to Fowey to meet the author. There was an instant attraction and, within a few weeks, the pair were engaged. The wedding took place at Lanteglos church opposite Fowey in July 1932, the bride and groom making their way to church by boat, up Pont Creek.

By now, Daphne was working on her next two novels, *I'll Never Be Young Again* and *The Progress of Julius*, neither of which quite fulfilled the promise of her first work. But she had no time to dwell on disappointment; she was pregnant with her first child, Tessa, and her father, by now Sir Gerald, was deteriorating in health. In April 1934, at the age of sixty-one and on his 31st wedding anniversary, he died. Six months later, Daphne published a biography of her father entitled *Gerald: A Portrait*. In it, she described him as 'a creature of contradictions, so old in experience, so young in wisdom – a child in the morning, a blasphemer at night.' The forthright nature of the book shocked some of Gerald du Maurier's adoring fans and critics labelled it 'staggeringly candid' and 'a merciless tribute'. In truth, however, the book was a refreshingly honest portrait of a complex character.

Maxim takes breakfast in Monte Carlo with his future bride.

Her husband's blossoming army career meant that he was frequently posted abroad and the newlyweds moved house no fewer than five times in six years. Daphne began to yearn for Cornwall and found that the only way to satisfy her longing was to recapture its glory in print. This she did via her fourth novel, and the most successful to date, *Jamaica Inn*, published in 1936.

The inspiration for the book had come from one of her many exploratory visits around Cornwall in the early Thirties. One day, in the company of her friend Foy Quiller-Couch (daughter of writer Sir Arthur Quiller-Couch), Daphne set off on horseback to visit an elderly lady who lived at Trebartha Hall on the edge of the wild, remote Bodmin Moor. As the weather closed in and the terrain became rougher, they were forced to seek refuge for the night and eventually found it at Jamaica Inn, high on the moor at Bolventor. The next day, they visited the moorland village of Altarnun where they became friendly with the local parson. As he regaled them with the dark legends of Bodmin Moor, the idea for a ripping yarn was born, coupled with the fact that, at the time, Daphne had just started reading *Treasure Island*. Seeing the parson with his long white hair, Daphne found it easy to imagine him as the sinister ringleader of a gang of smugglers, the role he was to undertake in the book.

> ... they were forced to seek refuge for the night and eventually found it at Jamaica Inn, high on the moor at Bolventor.

Jamaica Inn became so successful that it was subsequently made into a film by Alfred Hitchcock, who had worked with Gerald du Maurier when the latter had turned his talents to the cinema. The 1939 film of *Jamaica Inn* starred Charles Laughton, with Maureen O'Hara as the orphaned heroine Mary Yellan, but the adaptation did not meet with the author's approval. When Daphne du Maurier saw the end product at a London cinema she 'nearly wept', remarking 'about all that was left was the title.' Many of the problems arose from the American film censors, who insisted that a vicar could not be portrayed as a wrong-doer, so Laughton's character became a Justice of the Peace. Nevertheless the film did du Maurier's reputation no harm.

In the early years of her marriage, Daphne barely stopped writing. As soon as one project was finished, she began work on another. Her versatility had already demonstrated itself with her biography of her father and once again she turned to family history for *The du Mauriers*, chronicling their life in the nineteenth century.

In 1936 'Tommy' Browning was posted to Alexandria in Egypt as Commanding Officer of the Second Battalion, Grenadier Guards. Daphne went with him but returned to England the following year to give birth to their second daughter, Flavia, named after the princess in *The Prisoner of Zenda*. Then it was back to Egypt where Daphne reluctantly joined in the usual round of dinner parties attended by officers' wives. But her heart was still in Cornwall and, in particular in a house she had stumbled across shortly after her parents had bought Ferryside.

In an old guidebook to the area, Daphne and Angela found the name of a house built during the reign of Elizabeth I. It was called Menabilly and was to dominate Daphne du Maurier's life for nearly forty years.

Daphne was determined to take a closer look and so, one afternoon, accompanied by Angela and their friend Mary Fox (aunt of actors Edward and James Fox), they set off for Menabilly. The house was some three miles from Fowey Harbour

and could only be reached by way of a long, winding, overgrown drive. As the three trespassers entered the grounds through creaky iron gates, past the deserted lodge and ploughed through clumps of rhododendron bushes, the eeriness of the place began to affect Angela, who grew distinctly uneasy. But Daphne was captivated by it. She later described the experience in *The Rebecca Notebook & Other Memories*: 'It had the magic quality of a place hitherto untrodden, unexplored... The woods were sleeping now, but who, I wondered, had ridden through them once? What hoofbeats had sounded and then died away? What carriage wheels had rolled and vanished? Doublet and hose. Boot and jerkin. Patch and powder. Stock and patent leather. Crinoline and bonnet. The trees grew taller and the shrubs more menacing. Yet still the drive led on, and never a house at the end of it.'

> ...the place had been left to decay – windows were broken, the shutters were hanging loose and the walls were caked in fungus...

Angela's reluctance, coupled with the failing light, persuaded them to abandon the mission temporarily but Daphne never forgot the mysterious house. She knew she would be back one day.

The weather prevented any further investigation that autumn but the family returned to Cornwall the following spring. One day Daphne was out fishing in a boat in Pridmouth Bay when she spotted the roof of a house peering through the trees on the densely wooded hillside leading down to the water. She asked the boatman what it was and he replied 'Menabilly'. Seized once again with the desire to find the elusive house, she rose early the following morning, rowed across the harbour and took a different route up through the woods. Eventually she came upon the neglected old house, covered in ivy. Peering through the gloomy windows, she saw furniture gathering dust, stacks of paintings and a children's rocking-horse. 'The house possessed me from that day,' she wrote, 'even as a mistress holds her lover.'

Further enquiries revealed Menabilly to be the property of a Dr Rashleigh although he rarely lived there. After that initial voyage of discovery, Daphne visited Menabilly whenever possible, wandering in the grounds for hours, with the owner's permission, trying to imagine how the house must have been in its heyday and what life must have been like there for generations of Rashleighs. She began investigating the Rashleigh family history and found it steeped in colour and intrigue. Both Menabilly and the Rashleighs were to provide key elements for her next novel, *Rebecca*. The book and the film adaptation, starring Laurence Olivier, were to make both *Rebecca* and Daphne du Maurier household names. Her next work, the historical romance *Frenchman's Creek*, also took its inspiration from an area of Cornwall, this time the Helford River which Daphne had first visited during her honeymoon. The film rights to *Frenchman's Creek* were sold to Paramount Pictures for £30,000, and starred Joan Fontaine (who had played the heroine in *Rebecca)*, Arturo de Cordova and Basil Rathbone.

Although 'Tommy' Browning was heavily occupied with the war (he was promoted to Lieutenant-General in 1944), he and Daphne spent sufficient time together to produce a third child, a son Christian. While pregnant, she wrote *Hungry Hill*, a story about a long-standing family feud set in Ireland, rather than Cornwall, although the background history was relayed to her by an Irish friend who lived in Fowey. This too was to become a film featuring Margaret Lockwood

Maxim with his faithful dog, Jasper.

Opposite:
Maxim de Winter
(Charles Dance).

and Dennis Price.

Hungry Hill appeared in print in 1943 and that same year Daphne took the opportunity to visit Menabilly for the first time since the outbreak of war. She had been previously notified by Angela that there was to be a sale of the entire contents of the old house. Daphne would have liked to have bought the lot but it was not practical and anyway what she wanted more than anything was to buy the house itself. But both the house and the estate were entailed, rendering that particular dream an impossibility. Nevertheless she was so angry about the way in which the place had been left to decay – windows were broken, the shutters were hanging loose and the walls were caked in fungus and mould – that she contacted her lawyer and asked him to write to the Rashleighs to ascertain whether there was any chance of her leasing Menabilly. A week later she was delighted to be told that she could have a twenty-five-year lease on the house.

Restoring Menabilly to anything remotely resembling its former glory was no small task. There was no electricity, no water, no heating and the roof had caved in at certain points. People thought she was mad to undertake such a restoration but, through her books, Daphne du Maurier was by now sufficiently wealthy to be able to buy the impossible, even in wartime. Nine months later Menabilly was unrecognisable, splendidly refurbished just in time for her husband's Christmas leave.

In September 1944, Browning's reputation took a battering following the ill-fated Arnhem landings. Field Marshal Montgomery had prepared Operation 'Market Garden' to secure five bridges on the Rhine, to enable the Allied armies to advance north. The northernmost bridge was at Arnhem in Holland. Browning had grave reservations and declared prophetically: 'I think we may be going a bridge too far.' But he was tremendously loyal to Montgomery and, unable to resist such a powerful character, went along with the plan, never again expressing any misgivings. The mission was a disaster, with over 17,000 Allied soldiers killed or

The production team
get ready to roll the
cameras.

wounded. Only a few of those who held Arnhem Bridge lived to tell the tale. Word reached Daphne that her husband had been among those captured but happily this proved a false alarm. Nevertheless she had to endure an agonising twenty-four-hour wait before learning that he was safe. Browning, who was in charge of the airborne operation, took much of the blame and the incident haunted him until his death in 1965. When Richard Attenborough made the film *A Bridge Too Far* (in which Browning was played by Dirk Bogarde) in 1975, Daphne was incensed about what she perceived as the negative portrayal of her late husband who had enjoyed distinguished service in both world wars. 'They were looking for a fall guy,' she bridled. 'My God, they wouldn't have dared if Boy had been alive. He would have roasted them.'

> Her husband's royal connections meant that Daphne was required to attend social functions at Buckingham Palace...

Ensconced in her dream home, Daphne continued to write copiously throughout the war, penning a succession of short stories and then another historical novel, *The King's General*. The idea was prompted by reading a book on the English Civil War and by the papers of the Rashleigh family who were involved in it. Legend had it that a skeleton dating from that era had been discovered at Menabilly in the nineteenth century when a new kitchen wing was being added to the house. Writing the book in surroundings steeped in history, Daphne's vivid imagination ran riot and she even featured the house as a setting. She also worked on two plays, *The Years Between*, which opened in London in 1945 to moderate reviews and the romantic *September Tide* which opened in 1948 and starred her friend Gertrude Lawrence.

Meanwhile rumours were circulating about the state of her marriage. The lengthy wartime separations inevitably put a strain on relationships and fuelled gossip. Browning had had a relationship before they were married and now there was talk that he had a mistress in London. She dedicated *The King's General* 'To my husband, also a General, but, I trust, a more discreet one!' It has been suggested by at least one biographer of Daphne du Maurier that Browning took exception to the wording of the dedication, but this was simply not true. On the contrary, he was quite amused by it. Nevertheless, it was not until the war was over that their marriage got back on an even keel.

In 1948, Browning resigned from the army and, on Mountbatten's recommendation, was appointed Comptroller of the Household of the newly-married Princess Elizabeth. Daphne du Maurier was at the height of her fame, working at Menabilly from what she called her 'hut at the bottom of the garden', with a spectacular view out across the English Channel. After planning the storyline and characters, often over a period of several months, she would jot down a short synopsis for each chapter. At the writing stage, she would spend six days a week in the 'hut', thrashing away at her old typewriter between puffs of cigarettes, the routine broken only by meals and a post-lunch stroll to the cliffs with her West Highland terriers. To the dismay of her publishers, she could never guarantee when her next book would appear – she detested writing to order. She cheerfully admitted that her grammar was poor and her spelling abysmal. Although she owned a dictionary, she could never be bothered to look up words, relying instead on her editor to make any corrections. But every du Maurier book was a sure-fire bestseller.

For her next novel, *The Parasites*, she chose a London setting and that of a theatrical family, the Delaneys, who were clearly based on the du Mauriers. She later remarked that the three leading characters, Maria, Niall and Celia, were all reflections of herself, a rare attempt at self-analysis. She returned to a Menabilly location for her 1951 success *My Cousin Rachel*, using a young male narrator, Philip, to guide the reader through a tale of Cornish murder and mystery. The inevitable film starred a young Richard Burton as Philip with Olivia de Havilland as the enigmatic Rachel, although Daphne herself had envisaged Vivien Leigh in the role.

In 1952, a collection of Daphne du Maurier's short stories was published under the title *The Apple Tree*. Here readers saw her in a very different light, as the stories take on a sinister, macabre aspect. The most famous was *The Birds*, inspired by a walk across a ploughed field to Menabilly Barton farm. Seagulls were circling and diving noisily overhead and she took to imagining the result if birds suddenly became hostile to man. It later became one of Hitchcock's most celebrated films, although Daphne was disappointed that the story was uprooted from Cornwall to America.

After penning *Mary Anne*, the story of her great-great-grandmother Mary Anne Clarke, du Maurier wrote *The Scapegoat*, a murder mystery about an unassuming Englishman who meets his double, a French aristocrat. Alec Guinness starred in the film version.

Her husband's royal connections meant that Daphne was required to attend social functions at Buckingham Palace, Sandringham and Balmoral. This she did with great reluctance – preferring to lounge around her beloved Menabilly in a pair of slacks. Neither was she keen on entertaining guests although the Queen and Prince Philip were among the visitors to Menabilly.

By now, Daphne had begun to retreat increasingly into her private world. She rarely gave interviews to promote her books and other writers described her as

Maxim enjoys the girl's company and the scenery of the south of France.

'hiding behind the seclusion of Menabilly with its rhododendron screen' and as living a 'hermit-like existence'.

Her mother Muriel, to whom she had grown much closer, died in 1956 and towards the end of the decade, the health of 'Tommy' also began to deteriorate. He retired from the Royal Service through ill health in 1959 and was thereafter able to spend more time with Daphne at Menabilly. It was clear in their last years together that the strength of their relationship was that they genuinely liked each other and were intensely proud of each other's achievements.

With Daphne du Maurier achieving so much distinction as a novelist, it is easy to overlook the fact that she was also a perceptive biographer, as shown by her portrait of her father. She had always acknowledged the debt she owed the Brontës and decided to write a biography of the forgotten Brontë, their brother Branwell, who had strong Cornish connections. *The Infernal World of Branwell Brontë*, was published in 1961.

Daphne's output became more sporadic during the Sixties (*The Glass-Blowers* [1963], *The Flight of the Falcon* [1965] and *The House on the Strand* [1969]), a decade marked by two body-blows. On the death of Dr Rashleigh, the Menabilly estate passed to his nephew Phillip who announced that he wanted to return and live in the house and would therefore not be extending Daphne's lease. Daphne made public her feelings about being forced out of her home and Phillip Rashleigh felt obliged to offer her alternative accommodation, the Rashleigh Dower House, in Kilmarth, which overlooked Par Bay. Despite his own failing health, not helped by the fact that he had become a heavy drinker, 'Tommy' strove to soften the blow of the impending move. 'I like this place,' he said of Kilmarth. 'I can see ourselves here.' Sadly, he never lived to discover whether his prediction was correct. He died on 14 March 1965 from a sudden coronary thrombosis. To overcome her grief, Daphne took to wearing his shirts, wrote at his desk and answered letters from well-wishers with his pens.

The death of her husband made the loss of Menabilly even more unbearable. The writing of *Vanishing Cornwall*, a non-fiction book about her favourite county, helped ease the pain but it could not postpone the inevitable and eventually she moved out of Menabilly in the summer of 1969, ending twenty-six glorious years.

Two years later, her publishers, Victor Gollancz, brought out another anthology of supernatural short stories, *Not After Midnight*. Among the tales was *Don't Look Now*, later turned into a successful film starring Donald Sutherland and Julie Christie. The idea for the story had come to Daphne while on holiday in Venice with her son Christian, affectionately known as Kits. Even in her sixties, Daphne du Maurier retained an eye for a good plot and an impeccable sense of place. Few people wrote better about locations.

In the spring of 1969 Daphne was made a Dame. She grew increasingly solitary throughout the Seventies, rarely venturing out of her adopted county and was at her most content walking her dogs along the coastal path near Kilmarth. Whilst she did not encourage attention from members of the public, she was never rude to them. 'I can't say I really like people,' she once commented. 'Perhaps that's why I always preferred to create my own instead of mixing with real ones.'

Her final novel, *Rule Britannia*, was published in 1972 and was dedicated to the actress Gladys Cooper. A political satire with strong overtones of Cornish independence, *Rule Britannia* was a complete departure from the norm for du Maurier and one which left her faithful readership thoroughly baffled. She also produced two biographies about Francis Bacon and his set as well

as finally giving in to pressure to write her autobiography, *Growing Pains*, although this only covered her life up until her marriage.

Maxim (Charles Dance) points out Manderley to his second wife (Emilia Fox).

She made a rare venture out of Cornwall in the autumn of 1981 for a holiday in Scotland with her son. She hoped that it would provide inspiration for a further novel, but any hopes in that direction were dashed the following year when she suffered what was described at the time as a severe nervous breakdown. Her inability to write made her increasingly depressed and awkward. She became ever more reclusive and began to lose her memory. By the time of her death, on 19 April 1989, at the age of eighty-one, she had little knowledge of what was going on around her.

It was a sad end for one of the most inventive minds in modern literature. Fortunately, in the shape of her twenty-five full-length books and numerous short stories, Daphne du Maurier has left a golden legacy to millions of readers throughout the world.

*Maxim and the second
Mrs de Winter listen
as the news is broken
to them about
Rebecca.*

Chapter Two

The Road to Manderley

In 1937 Daphne du Maurier was already an established author, with four novels to her name as well as two family biographies. She had been married for five years and had two young daughters, the second still a baby. Besides her family, she had another love, Cornwall and, in particular, Menabilly, the ramshackle old house which she had discovered near Fowey. Yet in the autumn of that year, she found herself far from the house of her dreams, in Egypt dutifully accompanying her soldier husband who was commanding officer of the Second Battalion, Grenadier Guards, stationed in Alexandria.

The children had stayed behind in England, cared for by the family nanny, and Daphne and 'Tommy' Browning were living in a rented beach house at Ramleh. While he was busy attending to military affairs, Daphne found herself with time on her hands, a tedium scarcely broken by the seemingly interminable round of regiment cocktail parties which she was obliged to attend. She grew homesick for Cornwall and decided that if she was unable to be there in person, the next best thing was to write about it. This time, instead of writing a historical novel like *Jamaica Inn*, she wanted to set her story in the present day.

> 'a rather sinister tale about a woman who marries a widower... Psychological and rather macabre.'

She had told her publisher, Victor Gollancz, that she would start writing again in August of that year, four months after the birth of Flavia, and hinted that it might be 'a rather sinister tale about a woman who marries a widower... Psychological and rather macabre.' As with all of Daphne du Maurier's great works, a sense of place is crucial to the success of the novel. For this latest book, she chose an old Cornish house, located in extensive grounds, with rhododendron-filled woods, close to the sea – a house that had been lived in by the same family for generations. The similarity to Menabilly and the Rashleighs is immediately apparent, yet whilst the location was clearly based on Menabilly, the house itself was not. The fictional house, Manderley, owes more to a larger house, Milton, near Peterborough, the ancestral home of the Fitzwilliam family and a place where Daphne du Maurier had stayed as a child during the First World War.

To this day, controversy rages among *Rebecca* aficionados as to whether Menabilly or Milton is the real Manderley but the truth is that Manderley is a combination of the two. Daphne's memory of the rooms at Milton, and particularly the family portraits which adorned the walls, were recalled in her description of the interior of Manderley. The entrance halls of Milton and Manderley are also

The crew on location in the south of France.

identical, apart from the sweeping staircase which du Maurier invented for dramatic effect. Her idea was that Manderley would be empty and neglected, with its owner frequently absent, a striking similarity to Menabilly under the ownership of Dr Rashleigh. Yet when du Maurier visited Milton, parts of that house too lay idle. The furniture in some rooms was covered in dustsheets, the same sight which greeted the second Mrs de Winter as she explored Manderley in *Rebecca*. There is also a possibility that the forbidding housekeeper of Manderley, Mrs Danvers, may have been partly based on a Miss Parker who occupied the same post at Milton in 1917. She was described by Lady Fitzwilliam as 'tall, dark, brooding and very commanding', and Daphne du Maurier herself remembered Miss Parker as a 'severe and rather frightening person'. However the author was at great pains to add that the truly sinister side of Mrs Danvers' character was purely a creation of her imagination.

The Menabilly links extend beyond the grounds to the beach house in the cove on Polridmouth (or Pridmouth) Bay. This building became the beach cottage below Manderley where Rebecca was murdered. The wreck of Rebecca's boat was also found in the bay, mirroring a real-life event shortly after Daphne du

Maurier's first visit to Fowey when she walked across to Pridmouth Bay and saw a boat wrecked on the beach. Such images remained in her head to be used at a later date.

Daphne du Maurier envisaged her central characters in *Rebecca* as being a young wife and a slightly older husband. Fleshing out the characters, she recalled how her friends the Quiller-Couches had told her that Dr Rashleigh, the owner of Menabilly, had married a beautiful wife whom he had divorced before marrying a girl much younger than himself. Du Maurier began to wonder whether the second wife was ever jealous of the first.

> ...all she wanted to think about was the development of the plot.

A similar theme was pursued much closer to home. Not long after her wedding, Daphne had chanced upon a bundle of letters in her husband's desk. They were from Jan Ricardo, a woman to whom 'Tommy' Browning had once been engaged. Jan Ricardo was strikingly beautiful, witty and confident, and her love letters were written in a suitably bold hand. As Daphne read the letters, her guilt at prying into her husband's personal belongings was mixed with a strange feeling of inadequacy and insecurity. Jan Ricardo seemed to her to have all the things she lacked, and the realisation that 'Tommy' had loved another troubled her greatly. Perhaps she felt threatened in the same way that Dr Rashleigh's second wife may have been; in the same way that the second Mrs de Winter would be. Daphne later wrote of her husband's former love: 'Perhaps she would have been better at dinners and cocktail parties than I could ever be.'

Thus the outgoing, self-assured Jan Ricardo almost certainly became the role model for the character of Rebecca, with the young, quiet, self-effacing second Mrs de Winter based to a considerable extent upon Daphne du Maurier herself. Actress Joan Fontaine, who played the second Mrs de Winter in Hitchcock's film version of *Rebecca*, said that Daphne du Maurier had once admitted to her that she was the girl in the story. As for Maxim de Winter, the husband, some scribes insist he is based solely on 'Tommy' Browning, others that he is a mixture of Browning and Daphne's father, Gerald du Maurier. If Daphne had a particular person in mind, she never let on.

At first, progress on the book was painfully slow, not helped by the stifling Egyptian heat. She had hoped to deliver the finished manuscript in December but had to tell Victor Gollancz that the way things were going, there was little prospect of that deadline being met. All she had was a provisional title, *Rebecca*, and some scribbled notes which read: 'Very roughly the book will be about the influence of a first wife on a second... she is dead before the book opens. Little by little I want to build up the character of the first in the mind of the second... until wife 2 is haunted day and night.'

The first 15,000 words were thrown away (Daphne citing 'a literary miscarriage') but now, steadily, the elements of the new book began to fall into place – the beautiful home, the first wife, the jealousy, the shipwreck. But somewhere along the line an awful event had to have taken place. Daphne later described how she paced up and down the living room in Alexandria, notebook in hand, chewing first her nails and then her pencil as she searched for that missing ingredient. She cursed the fact that she had to go out to dinner that night when all she wanted to think about was the development of the plot.

Over the following few days, the ideas flowed thick and fast. The couple would

be living abroad – a situation with which du Maurier herself was all too familiar – in the wake of a tragedy. She also contemplated a literary device which she had never previously used – that of starting at the end of the story and then going back in time to work towards it again. She listed five essential guidelines which she was to follow during the writing of the book – atmosphere; simplicity of style; keep to the main theme; characters few and well defined; and build it up little by little. She began outlining the plot in her notebook, dividing everything up into chapters, twenty-six in all, plus the provision for an epilogue. Thus the evocative picture of Cornwall was not constructed while overlooking Fowey Harbour as many readers must have imagined, but hundreds of miles away in Egypt.

The storyline was then put on hold for a few months until she and 'Tommy' returned to England in mid-December. They rented an old house called Greyfriars, near Fleet in Hampshire ('Tommy' was stationed at Aldershot), installed the children and household staff and then, when the necessary order around her was restored, Daphne returned to the notes she had made in Egypt. Soon *Rebecca*, the classic tale which was to be translated into more than twenty languages, was flowing from her typewriter. Above all, Daphne du Maurier succeeded in entering the mind of her heroine to such an extent that she could create a picture of the fantasy world in which the second Mrs de Winter lived. The novel opens with a dream and retains a dream-like structure whereby the reader is constantly drawn into the heroine's haunted imagination. What happens in the girl's mind becomes more important than the events which take place around her.

The story of *Rebecca* is told by its heroine, the second Mrs de Winter. Once a socially inept, somewhat naïve girl, she is now a middle-aged wife living in the south of France with her older husband, Maxim, a man still suffering pain from the aftermath of a serious fire. She recounts the events that brought them there, remembering how they had first met on holiday in Monte Carlo where she was acting as the paid companion to a rich, vulgar American woman, Mrs Van Hopper. The girl was not the most elegant of creatures. She wore her hair in a plain, straight, bobbed style and was dressed in an ill-fitting coat and skirt and a jumper of her own creation. She would trail in the wake of Mrs Van Hopper 'like a shy, uneasy colt'.

Seeing Maxim de Winter, Mrs Van Hopper, with her 'fat, bejewelled fingers', pounces on him and begins interrogating him about his absence from the family home of Manderley in Cornwall. The girl recalls how the insensitive Mrs Van Hopper 'ran on like a clumsy goat, trampling and trespassing on land that was preserved.' Her prying puts Maxim on edge and he leaves abruptly. But when Mrs Van Hopper is laid low with influenza, he sees the opportunity to engage the girl in conversation and to show a more tender side to his nature. She begins to feel at ease with him and reveals how she is an orphan. Her parents (her father was an artist) had died within five weeks of each other.

The girl finds herself instantly attracted to the sophisticated Maxim and learns that he is a widower after his beautiful wife, Rebecca, had been drowned in a sailing accident. To the girl's amazement, Maxim becomes equally infatuated with her. Following a whirlwind romance, he proposes marriage, much to the disgust of Mrs Van Hopper, who tells the girl she is making a fool of herself. 'You can scarcely string two sentences together at my bridge teas, what are you going to say to all his friends?' She informs the girl that Maxim only wants her because he is lonely in that big house. 'You haven't flattered yourself he's in love with you?'

However the marriage goes ahead and Maxim takes her back to Manderley.

Opposite:
Love grows between
Maxim and the naïve
young girl.

The long drive at Manderley twists and turns and seems to go on forever until at last they come to the house. The new bride is understandably nervous and is handicapped by her gaucherie, yet she is desperately eager to please. But her inexperience counts against her and she finds herself ill-equipped to cope with her position as mistress of the household, particularly when confronted by the sinister housekeeper, Mrs Danvers, a tall, gaunt woman dressed in black 'whose prominent cheek bones and great, hollow eyes gave her a skull's face.' Mrs Danvers wastes little time in revealing how devoted she was to Rebecca. She even keeps the rooms once frequented by Rebecca, notably the bedroom in the west wing overlooking the sea, exactly as they had been when she was alive. Not surprisingly, the girl feels intimidated by Mrs Danvers and barely fit to follow in Rebecca's noble footsteps.

Every minor incident seems like a test. When, alone in the drawing-room, she answers the telephone and hears that the call is for Mrs de Winter, she instinctively blurts out that there must be a mistake – Mrs de Winter has been dead for over a year. It is only then that she realises that *she* is now Mrs de Winter. To make matters worse, the caller is Mrs Danvers, who would be sure to capitalise on such vulnerability.

Maxim and his second wife on the drive to Manderley.

Maxim's friends and relations, notably his sister Beatrice (broad-shouldered, tweedy and horsey), her husband Giles and family acquaintance Frank Crawley, do their best to make the new Mrs de Winter feel at home, but she remains convinced that she is living in the shadow of Rebecca. While exploring the grounds of Manderley with Maxim's dog Jasper, the narrator discovers a beach cottage and gets talking to a harmless simpleton by the name of Ben. Maxim is uneasy when he discovers that she has been near the cottage. He tells her that he never goes near the beach or the cottage and hints that the place holds bad memories. To his wife's chagrin, he declares that he thinks he has made a terrible mistake in bringing her back to Manderley.

All the locals seem to be comparing her to Rebecca. She decides that the best way to deal with the situation is to discuss Rebecca openly. In conversation with the bishop's wife, she suddenly finds herself saying that Rebecca must have been a wonderful person. It is as if a huge weight has been lifted from her shoulders. 'I could not believe that I had said the name at last... It was as though I had taken a purge and rid myself of an intolerable pain.'

The girl is anxious to learn more about the mysterious Rebecca and begins to

Over tea Maxim's sister Beatrice (Geraldine James) gets acquainted with the second Mrs de Winter.

The second Mrs de Winter probes Frank Crawley (Tom Chadbon) about Rebecca.

probe Frank Crawley. He tells her that Rebecca drowned when her boat capsized in the bay and she was washed overboard. Her body was found two months later, forty miles away near Edgecombe. The girl wants to know more but Crawley is too diplomatic to enter into great detail.

The darkness surrounding Rebecca deepens when the girl once again bumps into Ben who reveals how Rebecca used to entertain friends at the beach cottage. Trembling for fear of being thrown into an asylum, he insists that he had never previously told this to anyone. It transpires that he was terrified of Rebecca, who had threatened him if she caught him looking at her through the windows of the cottage. Clearly Rebecca wasn't such a saint after all.

Meanwhile Mrs Danvers continues to undermine the new Mrs de Winter at every turn, making her ever more uncomfortable and unhappy. Her fragile confidence is jolted yet further when she accidentally breaks a tiny china cupid, a favourite family heirloom. Riddled with guilt, she scoops the fragments into an envelope but when Maxim is alerted to its disappearance and the staff are being blamed, she is forced to confess. Happily, Maxim is in a forgiving mood.

The girl is introduced to Jack Favell, Rebecca's cousin, a heavy-drinker and womaniser who strongly hints that there was more to Rebecca's death than meets the eye. There is evidently a great deal of ill-feeling between Favell and Maxim. Mrs Danvers offers to show the girl Rebecca's room. The girl becomes unnerved by the housekeeper's obsession with the late mistress and notes that Mrs Danvers' eyes seemed malevolent, full of hatred. Mrs Danvers goes so far as to wonder whether Rebecca returns to Manderley to watch Maxim and the girl together. The spirit of

Rebecca looms larger still when Beatrice takes the girl to meet Maxim's grand-
mother who immediately demands to know why Rebecca isn't there.

    Still desperate to make an impression, the girl sees the forthcoming fancy
dress ball (an event for which Manderley has long been famous) as the opportunity
to show Maxim that she can be the equal of Rebecca. She has long admired a portrait in the house of a lady dressed all in white – it is of Caroline de Winter, a sister of Maxim's great-great-grandfather. Now, acting on the advice of Mrs Danvers,
the girl decides to wear a similar costume to the ball. When she descends the stairs
in the dress, the assembled guests fall into stunned silence. Maxim is livid and
orders her to get changed. Unknowingly, she is wearing exactly the same dress that
Rebecca had worn at the last fancy dress ball before her death. As she runs off in
tears, the girl passes Mrs Danvers. 'I shall never forget the expression on her face,
loathsome, triumphant. The face of an exulting devil.'

    Maxim thinks his new wife has deliberately copied Rebecca while the girl her-
self is utterly distraught, convinced that her husband has never got over the tragic
loss of his first wife. Mrs Danvers seizes on the girl's increased vulnerability, telling
her that she is not wanted at Manderley and that she should leave Maxim to be
alone with his memories of Rebecca. The girl challenges Mrs Danvers about the
dress, saying how the episode has hurt Maxim. Mrs Danvers promptly declares that
she doesn't care about Maxim, adding that he deserves to suffer for marrying a girl
only ten months after the death of 'my Mrs de Winter... the real Mrs de Winter'. As
the fog swirls outside, Mrs Danvers forces her towards the open window of
Rebecca's bedroom. Gripping her by the arm, the housekeeper snarls: 'Why don't

*Director, Jim O'Brien,
takes a closer look at
the action.*

you jump? It wouldn't hurt, not to break your neck... Don't be afraid. What's the use of your staying here at Manderley? You're not happy. Mr de Winter doesn't love you. There's not much for you to live for, is there? Why don't you jump now and have done with it? Then you won't be unhappy any more.' Just then, a fearful crashing sound shakes them both to their senses and Mrs Danvers calmly loosens her grip.

The noise was that of the rockets, denoting that a ship has been lost in the nearby bay. As divers plunge into the waters to investigate, they discover the wreck of another boat. It is Rebecca's yacht and her body is still in the cabin. This immediately turns the spotlight of suspicion upon Maxim who had previously identified another woman's body, found further up the coast, as being that of Rebecca. Maxim pours out his heart to his new wife, confessing that this second body is indeed Rebecca's. He says he had never really loved her – indeed he had come to hate her. She had taunted him about her affairs, saying that if she ever had a son, even if it wasn't Maxim's, he would still inherit Manderley because nobody would be able to prove who was the real father. Maxim recounts how, racked with jealousy and anger, he had shot Rebecca dead in the beach cottage. He had then taken her body to her boat, sailed it out to sea and sunk the vessel with her still on board. The girl vows to stand by her husband and to cover up for him if necessary.

Maxim and the second Mrs de Winter drive to Dr Baker's clinic in London.

The subsequent inquest hears evidence that the boat seemed to have been sunk deliberately. Three holes had been driven into the planking. Maxim is questioned about his relationship with his ex-wife, at which point the girl faints. Although there appears no obvious reason why Rebecca should have taken her own

life, a verdict of suicide is reached. But Favell in unconvinced. He admits that he and Rebecca were lovers and insists that Maxim killed Rebecca in a jealous rage. He produces an ambiguous note from Rebecca – the last thing she ever wrote to him – in which she urged him to meet her at the beach cottage as she had something of great importance to tell him. The suggestion is clear – that Rebecca was expecting Favell's child. Giving this as a motive for murder, the unscrupulous Favell attempts to blackmail Maxim who responds by knocking him to the ground.

Determined to bring about Maxim's downfall, Favell tries to persuade Mrs Danvers to tell the local magistrate, Colonel Julyan, that he (Favell) and Rebecca were in love. But Mrs Danvers dismisses the notion out of hand, stating bluntly that Rebecca was not in love either with Favell or Maxim. 'She despised all men,' announces Mrs Danvers. 'She was above all that.' To Favell's acute embarrassment, she goes on to reveal that Rebecca used to laugh out loud about her lovemaking with him. On the question of suicide, Mrs Danvers adds that the only thing Rebecca ever feared was a lingering death. She had always wanted to go quickly 'like the snuffing out of a candle'.

In desperation, the de Winters search through Rebecca's papers and find that on the day of her death she had an appointment under the name of Mrs Danvers with a Harley Street specialist, Dr Baker. Together with Favell and Colonel Julyan, they visit the doctor, who informs them that Rebecca had terminal cancer and a physical condition which meant that she would never have been able to have children. Thus Favell's theory falls apart and even he is forced to concede that Rebecca did, after all, have reason to commit suicide, although he is still by no means convinced that she actually did so.

> ...as Maxim's car nears Manderley, beyond the distant hills on the horizon they see a red glow in the sky 'like a splash of blood'.

While the de Winters contemplate the return journey to Cornwall, Favell telephones Mrs Danvers with the news. Before setting off, Maxim also makes a call, to Frank Crawley, who informs them that Mrs Danvers appears to have left Manderley in a hurry.

It is a long journey through the night and as Maxim's car nears Manderley, beyond the distant hills on the horizon they see a red glow in the sky 'like a splash of blood'. At first, they think it must be dawn but then they realise that it is too early and the glow is coming from the wrong direction – the west. Maxim realises that it is Manderley. For, convinced that Maxim was getting away with murder, Mrs Danvers has set fire to Manderley. If her lady cannot have it, no one else shall.

It is interesting to compare the finished novel with Daphne du Maurier's original outline for the plot of *Rebecca*. The most obvious differences are in the names of the characters. Du Maurier initially envisaged calling Maxim 'Henry', but thought the latter sounded too dull. Similarly, she planned to name Jack Favell 'Paul Astley' and Maxim's sister Beatrice was called Barbara. The heroine remained unnamed, something which has puzzled readers over the years. The author's response as to why the second Mrs de Winter never had a christian name was simple: 'I could not think of one, and it became a challenge in technique, the easier because I was writing in the first person.' Also, Mrs Danvers was far less evil in the original notes and it was not her idea that the second Mrs de Winter should wear the white dress for the fancy dress ball – it was simply a regrettable coincidence. Du Maurier maintained that she was unsure as to precisely why Mrs Danvers

*Crawley, the second
Mrs de Winter and
Frith (John Horsley)
watch in disbelief as
the fire engulfs
Manderley.*

became such an unpleasant character.

There are a few major differences in the two storylines. In the first version, the girl reacted to her husband's outburst at the ball by drinking the disinfectant Lysol in an attempt to commit suicide. And it was at that point that de Winter confessed to his wife that he had murdered Rebecca whereas in the final version, he waited until after Rebecca's body had been found in the wreck. The final change is the ending. In her first draft, Daphne du Maurier did not conceive a fire at Manderley. Instead as the de Winters returned from the London meeting, fearful that Rebecca might yet wreak the ultimate vengeance upon them both from the grave, and turned into the drive of the old house, a car came straight at them with blazing headlights. Henry swerved to avoid it but his efforts were in vain.

Du Maurier also wrote an epilogue to her first story which was to form the basis for chapter two of the finished book. In her original epilogue, the couple survived the car crash but led a rather tragic, routine existence at a small hotel in the south of France. The scarred and crippled Henry could only walk with the aid of sticks as a result of the crash while his wife had rather gone to seed and wore dark glasses to conceal eyes that had lost their sparkle. In spite of their circumstances, they were not unhappy and had sufficient money to live in relative comfort. As for Manderley, it had been sold and converted into a country club, complete with sun terrace, squash courts, swimming pool and golf course.

It took Daphne du Maurier four months to write *Rebecca*. Upon its

Admiring glances.

completion in April 1938, she was filled with the sort of self-doubt which gave rise to the character of her heroine. Would her publisher, Victor Gollancz, think the story stupid or too melodramatic? 'It's a bit on the gloomy side,' she wrote to him, 'and the psychological side may not be understood.' She added that she thought it was too grim 'to be a winner'. The manuscript was read by Norman Collins, the senior editor at Victor Gollancz, who reported back excitedly: 'It brilliantly creates a sense of atmosphere and suspense...The new Daphne du Maurier contains everything that the public could want.' So it was with some relief that the manuscript met with the approval of her publishers and, ultimately more importantly, that of her rapidly expanding readership.

On reading the new script himself, Victor Gollancz echoed his editor's enthusiasm and ordered an initial print run of 20,000. Whilst delighted by their response, Daphne also felt a shade nervous, as if suddenly bearing a huge burden of responsibility. She wrote to Gollancz saying that she was worried in case the book was 'an awful flop' for fear that he would lose a lot of money. Daphne also hoped to make some money from *Rebecca*. She had received an advance of £1,000 and was on a generous royalty deal of twenty per cent on UK sales up to 10,000 copies and 25 per cent on sales between 10,000 and 20,000. However she was very much aware that she was the breadwinner of the family, her husband's army pay amounting to just £1.17s.0d a day. 'It's a bit grim sometimes,' she admitted, 'when I think in the middle of the night how difficult it would be for us if my mind stopped working.'

Ever the romantic, Maxim sweeps the girl off her feet by taking her for a drive into the hills above the French Riviera.

Her fears were to prove unfounded. Published in August 1938, *Rebecca* sold sufficiently well to go into a number of reprints within the first twelve months. Later that same year, it was published by Doubleday in the United States where it was to sell two million copies over the next four years. For a book that was to become a classic, the reviews were curiously mixed. The *New York Times* hailed *Rebecca* as 'an outstanding novel. I couldn't put it down.' But the *Times* in London sneered: 'There is nothing in this book beyond the novelette' and went on to write of 'the freakishly constructed characters, their odd behaviour and Miss du Maurier's somewhat individual grammar.' The only character of which that particular critic seemed to approve was Mrs Danvers.

Unusually for an author, Daphne du Maurier could take criticism – it was flattery which made her wary. She also wanted people to understand what *Rebecca* was about, that it was a study in jealousy rather than a love story. Thus, although the *Sunday Times* deemed *Rebecca* to be 'a grand story', Daphne disapproved of the review as a whole because it described the book as 'romance in the grand tradition.' In her opinion, there was more hatred in the book than love.

In spite of any misgivings, the book became popular in high places. When, in September 1938, Prime Minister Neville Chamberlain flew to his infamous Munich meeting with Hitler in his quest for 'peace in our time', the chosen light reading in his briefcase was a copy of *Rebecca*.

As critics and readers alike began to dissect the novel, the relationship between Mrs Danvers and Rebecca (who had always called her 'Danny') was subjected to particularly close scrutiny. It is clear in the book that the housekeeper absolutely adored her late mistress but was there something more to their relationship? Were they lovers? And was that why Mrs Danvers was so hostile to the new Mrs de Winter? If there were lesbian undertones to *Rebecca*, Daphne du Maurier always kept her views to herself.

Shortly after the release of the film version of *Rebecca*, Daphne du Maurier was stunned to find herself accused of plagiarism... not once, but twice. The first claim was made by a Mrs Edwina Macdonald, who said that the plot of *Rebecca* was taken from a short story she had written some years previously, entitled *Blind Windows*. She announced her intention to sue Selznick International Pictures and the book's American publishers Doubleday Doran. Daphne had never heard of Mrs Macdonald or her book and when *Blind Windows* was subsequently despatched to her, she could see no similarity whatsoever between it and *Rebecca*, apart from the fact that both male heroes had been married twice. This was scarcely the basis for a law suit but Mrs Macdonald appeared determined to prove her point.

The case was first heard in a lower American court and, although Mrs Macdonald's claims were rejected, she appealed against the decision. The matter dragged on and on, even continuing after the redoubtable Mrs Macdonald's death in 1946 when her family took up the cudgel with equal enthusiasm. It was not until 1947 that the case was finally resolved. Daphne was reluctant to travel all the way to the United States on what she considered such a pointless issue and for the first hearing had merely supplied a sworn written affidavit along with the relevant documentation. But this time the Doubleday lawyer urged her to attend in person, explaining that a firm denial of plagiarism by the author on the witness stand was the surest way of defeating the law suit. Thus, accompanied by her two younger children and their nanny – Tessa, the eldest daughter, was at boarding school – Daphne set off on her maiden visit to America.

The notebook in which she had scribbled those first thoughts in Egypt back in 1937 was produced in evidence, but the prosecution unearthed a review of *Blind Windows* from the *Times Literary Supplement*, which Daphne admitted she read regularly, and argued that she could have read the story there. Daphne stood her ground and coped well with the probing cross-examination even though she considered it 'utterly degrading' to have to answer questions about her writing. She was also terrified that details of the background to *Rebecca* would all come out in court and therefore become public knowledge – in other words, that the book had been inspired by her jealousy over her husband's earlier relationship with Jan Ricardo. For such a determinedly private woman, this would have been too much to bear.

Quite correctly, the case was dismissed. Afterwards, Daphne gave the notebook to Ellen Doubleday as a memento. When Ellen died, nearly thirty years later, the notebook passed to her daughter Puckie, who in turn sent it back to Daphne. Re-reading it for the first time in so many years, she came up with the notion for *The Rebecca Notebook and Other Memories*, eventually published in 1981. A footnote to the American trip was that Daphne was seasick on the *Queen Mary* all the way back to England. It probably made her more reluctant than ever to leave Cornwall.

The second accusation of plagiarism never came to court, which in some ways was fortunate for Daphne because as she herself later admitted, the similarities to *Rebecca* were far greater than in the Macdonald case. That is not to say there was anything sinister afoot – it was simply a coincidence, an instance of two writers independently having the same idea.

The novel in question was *A Sucesora*, penned in the early 1930s by a Brazilian writer, Carolina Nabuco. The book was touted around English publishers before being printed in Brazil in 1934. Seven years later, the *New York Times* drew parallels between *A Sucesora* and *Rebecca*. The heroine of both books is a shy, mousy second wife with an older husband who, following their marriage, takes her back to the grand family home. There both wives are intimidated by decidedly unpleasant housekeepers. In each case, the heroine accidentally breaks an antique ornament which she subsequently tries to hide and there is a masked ball which

brings about a sensational dénouement. Whilst the house in *A Sucesora* does not burn down like Manderley, the young wife expresses the wish that it would. Furthermore, both books feature a domineering sister-in-law who bears a marked physical similarity to the husband and who sets out to educate the inexperienced young wife in worldly matters. Even the members of the respective household staffs are strangely alike. The *New York Times* concluded: 'So numerous are the parallels that one may find them on almost every page... About the only difference is that at the end of the Brazilian book the young wife discovers she is pregnant.'

Daphne du Maurier vehemently denied that she had ever heard of either Miss Nabuco or *A Sucesora*, and despatched an indignant letter to the *New York Times* concerning both this and the Macdonald claim. 'Would it not be possible,' she wrote, 'to let these two authoresses fight it out as to which of them wrote my book?'

Literary experts on both sides of the Atlantic sprang to du Maurier's defence, pointing out that the idea of a second wife haunted by the spectre of her beautiful predecessor was not exactly new in the world of romantic fiction and therefore could hardly be copyrighted. The differences in the endings of the two books were also highlighted. The Brazilian heroine emerged victorious while the de Winters were forced to live in exile.

Miss Nabuco never did take legal action, leaving Daphne du Maurier puzzled by the similarity between the two books. In the end, it was just one of those things, a case of pure coincidence which did nothing to harm the enormous worldwide success of *Rebecca* and its author.

Rebecca was to become Daphne du Maurier's most celebrated novel, something which never ceased to amaze her. As a rule, she avoided re-reading her books but such was the interest in *Rebecca* and so detailed were the questions she was repeatedly asked about it by fans, that she felt obliged to flick through it on occasions. Typically, any pride in her work was kept to herself and in later years she would modestly tell those who sought to praise her that she considered the story to be a little old-fashioned. The fact that *Rebecca* has stood the test of time and become a literary classic would seem to suggest that on this occasion, she was being unnecessarily hard on herself. But then Daphne du Maurier never was one for self-congratulation.

Opposite:
Maxim contemplates
problems past and
present. Is he to be
haunted forever by
the ghost of Rebecca?

The future Mrs de Winter sketching the beautiful French Riviera.

CHAPTER THREE

Rebecca on Stage and Screen

In the late Thirties, as now, the big Hollywood studios were always on the look-out for a bestselling novel which could be turned into a blockbuster movie. In May 1938 American producer David O Selznick was working on the adaptation of a book by Margaret Mitchell about a headstrong Southern girl in the wake of the American Civil War. It was called *Gone with the Wind*.

Meanwhile Selznick's assistant, Kay Brown, had been studying the success of the English publication of *Rebecca* and thought that it had all the right ingredients for a successful film. Her only reservation was that in the book Maxim de Winter, a self-confessed murderer, is seen to walk free. Under the strict rules of American movie censorship, ruthlessly enforced by the Hays Office, no murderer was allowed to go unpunished on screen. Brown wrote to Selznick: 'The book has good writing and dramatic scenes that lead into a rather hysterical plot. The fact that it is a melodrama isn't so much against it – after all, melodrama has been responsible for some box-office classics – but the fact that the hero definitely murders his first wife, no matter how understandable it is in the story, makes it difficult from the censorship angle. Aside from this there are good roles for Ronald Colman and Carole Lombard.'

Selznick read a synopsis of *Rebecca* and agreed that it had definite possibilities and that Ronald Colman would be ideal for the part of Maxim de Winter. However he was a little worried about the title. 'It is difficult to think of calling a picture *Rebecca*,' he said, 'unless it was made for the Palestine market.' Accordingly, Selznick tried to persuade Doubleday, the book's American publishers, to allow him to change the title. Despite their refusal, Selznick went ahead and bought the film rights to the book for some £10,000.

At the time, Alfred Hitchcock, fast emerging as the most influential British director, was under contract to Selznick Studios. After initially dismissing the book as humourless and too much of a Cinderella story, Hitchcock began to see *Rebecca* as the ideal follow-up to *Jamaica Inn*. However news of his proposed involvement did not go down well with Daphne du Maurier, who hated Hitchcock's film version of *Jamaica Inn*, considering her ugly, violent villains to have been turned into 'Peter Pan pirates'. Selznick felt obliged to reassure her. 'It is my intention,' he wrote, 'to do *Rebecca* and not some botched-up semi-original, as was done with *Jamaica Inn*.'

> Under the strict rules of American censorship...no murderer was allowed to go unpunished on screen.

Selznick and Hitchcock held a series of meetings to discuss the project, in particular as to how they might overcome problems associated with the first-person narrative. Selznick briefly considered showing the character of Rebecca on screen. When news of this reached Daphne du Maurier in England, she fired off a letter to Selznick, imploring him not to 'resurrect the dead wife.' She continued: 'My conviction is very strong that once this beautiful young woman is shown, the contrast between her and the rather plain and dull second wife would kill the latter.' Again, Selznick did his utmost to reassure her.

Hitchcock delivered his first draft of the screenplay in June 1939. Selznick was not impressed, expressing the view in no uncertain terms that Hitchcock had veered disastrously from the novel. Hitchcock went back to the drawing-board and this time, with the aid of other writers, came up with a screenplay that was sufficiently faithful to the original to satisfy both producer and author. The major departure from the book that ultimately featured in the film was caused by something which was beyond Selznick's control. The Hays Office refused to compromise over the murder storyline with the result that the murder of Rebecca had to be rewritten as an accident.

*The make-up depart-
ment apply the
finishing touches to
Emilia Fox.*

Jasper basks in the attention of the second Mrs de Winter.

By now, Ronald Colman was no longer in the running for the part of Maxim. He had initially been worried about portraying a murderer in case it upset his fans, and even the new, sanitised Maxim failed to win him over. Selznick and Hitchcock approached William Powell but he was unavailable, so Selznick turned to Laurence Olivier who had just enjoyed enormous success as the brooding Heathcliff in the film of *Wuthering Heights*. Ironically, he had first been employed by Hollywood because of his physical resemblance to Ronald Colman.

Now the search was on to find an actress to play the heroine, a part described by Selznick as 'the biggest plum in years, second only to Scarlett O'Hara.' Olivier's lover, Vivien Leigh, who had played Scarlett, wanted the part, but she was considered wrong for it, not least by the author. Margaret Sullivan was considered as were Olivia de Havilland and Loretta Young. Finally, acting on the advice of fellow director George Cukor, Selznick and Hitchcock chose de Havilland's sister, Joan Fontaine. To complete the line-up, Judith Anderson was cast as Mrs Danvers, George Sanders as Jack Favell, Gladys Cooper as Beatrice, Florence Bates as Mrs Van Hopper and Reginald Denny as Frank Crawley.

> In the finest traditions of Hollywood, Cornwall was transferred to California.

In the finest traditions of Hollywood, Cornwall was transferred to California. The exterior scenes of the Manderley estate were shot at Del Monte near the coast and the exterior beach scenes were filmed on Catalina Island. Manderley itself was nothing but a studio set.

Filming began on 8 September 1939, five days after the start of the Second World War. Consequently, there was considerable tension among the English members of the cast and this led to a great deal of friction on set. Olivier, in particular, was ill at ease, struggling to get to grips with the character of Maxim. He later wrote: 'I couldn't find the reality of the part. Joan Fontaine played the girl beautifully but I was never sure how much she was to be deceived, nor indeed how much the audience were to be deceived. When Joan wore a copy of Rebecca's dress, for example, was I meant to be cross or furiously angry? But why? What about?' Selznick, who had originally wanted to end the film with smoke rising from the burning Manderley to form a letter R but eventually settled for a bedroom close-up on a piece of R-shaped embroidery, also expressed doubts about Olivier's performance. 'His pauses and spacing in the scene with the girl in which she tells him about the ball are the most ungodly, slow and deliberate actions I've ever seen. It is played as though he were deciding whether or not to run for President instead of whether or not to give a ball.'

The majority of the critics disagreed and Olivier was nominated for an Academy Award for Best Actor. He lost to James Stewart in *The Philadelphia Story*. Joan Fontaine and Judith Anderson were also nominated, and *Rebecca* won the Academy Award for Best Picture. In view of her reaction to *Jamaica Inn*, perhaps an even greater accolade was that the film gained the seal of approval of Daphne du Maurier.

Despite being filmed in Hollywood, *Rebecca* was quintessentially English and as such held great appeal for audiences eager for any glimpse of the traditional England at a time when its way of life was being threatened by German aggressors. Indeed it was seen as something of a morale-booster in those dark, early years of the war. Churchill himself commented that the film achieved 'more for the war effort than a legion of seasoned troops.'

Even before the film appeared, Daphne du Maurier was asked to adapt *Rebecca* for the West End stage. It was a task she undertook with some trepidation because the theatre was still an alien medium to her and one which, despite her father's illustrious career, held little interest. She also found difficulty in maintaining the atmosphere and suspense of the piece without being able to resort to the heroine's monologues or describing the landscape. Dialogue was not her forte but she knuckled down to the job and introduced additional exchanges between Maxim and his sister and tried to heighten the most dramatic scenes. She was not entirely convinced by the end product, delivered in June 1939, but hoped that the acting would redeem it. In that respect, she decided that John Gielgud would be the ideal choice as Maxim, an offer he rejected in favour of a more classic part although he has since admitted that he regretted the decision.

Even without Gielgud at the helm, the play proved a tremendous success.

Tom Chadbon as Frank Crawley.

Owen Nares was eventually selected to play de Winter, with Celia Johnson as the girl and Margaret Rutherford as a suitably formidable Mrs Danvers. Ultimately, it was the Blitz which closed the play, the theatre being hit by a bomb. Among the items pulled from the rubble was a small bronze statue of Gerald du Maurier which Daphne had given to the cast for good luck.

The postwar years saw the expansion of television in Britain although, in 1947, a year after the resumption of the service, there were still fewer than 100,000 sets in the entire country. Television drama was live and studio-bound, frequently little more than the recreation of a West End play. Thus on 19 January 1947, the BBC broadcast Harold Clayton's 105-minute production of *Rebecca*, set in the hall at Manderley. Michael Hordern played Maxim de Winter, with Dorothy Gordon as the second wife and Dorothy Black as Mrs Danvers.

There were no such restrictions of set when the BBC returned to Manderley in January 1979 for a four-part production, dramatised by Hugh Whitemore, and directed by Simon Langton. Unable to gain permission to film at Menabilly, the team settled on Caerhayes Castle. This disappointed du Maurier as she considered it to be 'too turrety' for Manderley. Jeremy Brett was cast as Maxim, Joanna David as the girl and Anna Massey as Mrs Danvers. (By a remarkable coincidence, Joanna David's partner, Edward Fox, is the nephew of Mary Fox, Daphne's friend who went on that first expedition to Menabilly fifty years earlier. And now Joanna's daughter, Emilia Fox, plays the girl in the new ITV production of *Rebecca*). The production adhered closely to the book, and the performances and the authentic Cornish locations meant that it was well received by viewers and critics alike.

In total, the BBC has broadcast four radio adaptations of *Rebecca*. The first, produced by John Richmond, was transmitted on the Home Service in two parts on the evening of 9 August 1947. It starred Reginald Tate as Maxim, Dulcie Grey as the second Mrs de Winter and Nancy Price as Mrs Danvers. Nearly seven years later, on 27 January 1954, the Light Programme broadcast Lester Powell's adaptation which starred Richard Williams as Maxim, Ann Todd as Mrs de Winter and Enid Lorimer as Mrs Danvers. An all-star cast was aired on Radio 4 on Christmas Day 1975, headed by Richard Pasco (Maxim), Jane Asher (Mrs de Winter) and Flora Robson (Mrs Danvers). The most recent version aired on Radio 4 on 27 December 1989, with Christopher Cazenove, Janet Maw and Rosalie Crutchley.

Opposite:
Maxim de Winter and the second Mrs de Winter.

Perhaps the most unusual adaptation of *Rebecca* was as an opera, something which surprised Daphne du Maurier who found it difficult to envisage music being set to her novel. However, in 1982, Wilfred Josephs' composition was successfully broadcast on Radio 3, conducted by David Lloyd-Jones, the artistic director of Opera North. It proved so popular that it was revived five years later.

CHAPTER FOUR

The New *Rebecca*

The early Eighties witnessed a flurry of television interest in the works of Daphne du Maurier. Following the BBC's 1979 production of *Rebecca*, the Corporation screened an adaptation of *My Cousin Rachel* in March 1983 starring Geraldine Chaplin as Rachel. Two months later, ITV serialised *Jamaica Inn* in three parts with cast headed by Patrick McGoohan, Trevor Eve and Jane Seymour. The executive producer on *Jamaica Inn* was Hilary Heath, an ardent fan of Daphne du Maurier who now, fourteen years later, has realised her dream of bringing a new production of *Rebecca* to television.

'I'm a du Maurier freak,' admits Hilary Heath. 'I love her writing and I love Cornwall – it's such a romantic area. When I did *Jamaica Inn*, I worked closely with du Maurier's son Kits, who is the literary executor of her estate, and with Robin Lowe, who is the agent for that estate. We've remained friends ever since and they knew that I had always wanted to do *Rebecca*.

'To me, *Rebecca* is a marvellous portrait of love, jealousy and guilt. It is also a study of any woman marrying a much older man – a man with baggage. Any 21-year-old, like the heroine in the book, who marries someone twice her age is marrying someone with a past. The turning point for the second Mrs de Winter is when Maxim says: "I hated Rebecca, I love you." Until that point, she was a woman up against a ghost.'

Hilary Heath knew that with its powerful storyline, compelling characters and superb sense of atmosphere, *Rebecca* would make wonderful television. She already had the blessing of the du Maurier estate to proceed with the project but she needed to acquire the world rights. 'In the United States, the law altered on rights held in perpetuity to the US rights reverting 56 years after publication. The task was still to negotiate the rest of the world rights which were held by ABC. In turn, ABC part-owned Tele-münchen in Germany and so this was eventually to become a co-production with both America and Germany.

'I started in earnest at the beginning of 1995. The first and, as it transpired, only executive I approached in the UK was Jonathan Powell at Carlton. He was immediately interested and has been a fierce supporter of the production ever since.'

Heath and Powell talked at length about the proposal but it was not until the autumn of 1995 that things really took off. 'We coincided with the enormous success of the BBC's adaptation of *Pride and Prejudice*,' says Hilary Heath, 'as a result of which period drama was heavily in favour again.'

Television drama goes through phases of popularity. Following on the success of *The Forsyte Saga*, in the early Seventies, period drama was all the rage, with acclaimed productions such as *Upstairs, Downstairs, Elizabeth R* and *The Six Wives of Henry VIII*. But thereafter the trend was for contemporary drama and it was feared that after *Brideshead Revisited* (1981) and *The Jewel in the Crown* (1984), the days of costume drama were over. The cost was simply too prohibitive, causing British producers to shy away from the classics in favour of detective series. Admittedly some of these, (such as *Poirot, Miss Marple, Campion* and *Cadfael*), had a period feel, but it was not until *Pride and Prejudice* that most programme makers realised that there was still a huge market for quality adaptations of literary masterpieces. Nick Elliott, the ITV network drama chief, had observed the shifting trend and when *Rebecca* was offered to him at the same time that *Pride and Prejudice* was attracting so many plaudits, he grasped it with both hands, commissioning the production almost immediately.

> The turning point for the second Mrs de Winter is when Maxim says: "I hated Rebecca, I love you."

As a writer to adapt the du Maurier novel, Jonathan Powell suggested Arthur Hopcraft, with whom he had worked so memorably on the award-winning adaptation of John le Carré's *Tinker, Tailor, Soldier, Spy*.

Hilary Heath says: 'It was a hectic period for me but that all added to the excitement in a way. For all sorts of practicalities, including the need for the rhododendrons, which are such a part of Manderley, to be in bloom, I knew I needed to be shooting *Rebecca* no later than the beginning of June. And there I was at the start of the year with just the second draft scripts from Arthur Hopcraft. But the joy was that Arthur delivered wonderful scripts. If it hadn't been for him, *Rebecca* would not have happened for another year.'

Arthur Hopcraft is one of our foremost screenwriters, with a distinguished track record in the field of adapting classic novels. Aside from *Tinker, Tailor, Soldier, Spy*, he has dramatised such works as Dickens' *Hard Times* and *Bleak House*. 'When I was first approached by Hilary Heath, I had never read *Rebecca*,' says Hopcraft, 'but I had seen the film and I remembered the particularly striking scenes. So it was all new to me and that made the task all the more interesting. Obviously I then read the book and, to be honest, I found parts of it quite irritating. There was a degree of soppiness which was acceptable for 1938 but which I didn't think' would work now. Having said that, I was attracted to the superb story with its dramatic high points and the intriguing characterisation. So, in spite of my reservations, I agreed to do it, on condition that I could make certain modifications to the original.

'Daphne du Maurier is wonderful on atmosphere but a lot of the dialogue is terribly dated. Some of it is a bit Mills and Boonish. In the first half of the book, there is a lot of rather tedious stuff with the heroine going on about tea rituals. But if you plot out the emotional and dramatic high spots, there are plenty of peaks at which to aim. What I set out to do was to retain the essence of the book but to make

Opposite:
Executive Producer,
Jonathan Powell.

Maxim de Winter.

sections of it more interesting. The criticism of du Maurier has often been that she is better with descriptions than dialogue, and some of her best writing certainly does appear in her descriptive passages. So what I did was to convert some of her descriptions into dialogue, thereby ensuring that the adaptation would not be stepping away from the nature of the book.

'It was important to get the characters right and one of the changes I made was to the heroine herself, the unnamed second Mrs de Winter. I thought that for a modern-day audience, her character was too dowdy, too timid. I wanted to inject a little more spirit into her and to make her more attractive. I felt that the spirit was always there but that she had been a young girl waiting to flower.

'*Rebecca* is really a psycho-thriller, a romantic love story with dark overtones. It was important for me to get things moving from the start – the opening to the book is a bit slow – and to get the love story growing. In television, it is important to get the audience hooked from the start. At the same time, there had to be this sense of menace hovering in the background. For Maxim is acting a deception, concealing the dreadful secret that he has killed his first wife, and that gives him dangerously unpredictable mood swings which his new wife simply cannot understand. I had to keep Maxim's inexplicable, volatile moods going right up to the moment where he finally confesses to the heroine that he killed Rebecca. He couldn't suddenly have a personality change at that point. It all has to fit in with the characterisation.

'I also thought that the character of Mrs Van Hopper needed some fine tuning. She kicks the film off and, as such, is a vital character. I thought the

audience needed someone good to look at early on and so I rewrote parts of her character. In the book and in the Hitchcock film, she is a frumpy American widow but I thought she should be younger – a boozy fifty-year-old past her best.

'Sometimes you are on a hiding to nothing when adapting popular novels, because devotees of the author and the book will invariably disagree with some of the things you do. The trouble is that everyone has their own interpretation. If three friends go to a football match, they won't agree on a version of events; each will see things differently. So you can't expect the thousands of Daphne du Maurier fans to agree on one interpretation of *Rebecca*. The moment you cast someone to play a character from a book, you change it. People will say things like: "Why hasn't Maxim got a moustache?"

'There are certain things which people come to expect, however. In *Rebecca*, they will expect to hear the famous opening line to the book – "Last night I dreamt I went to Manderley again." I felt that line had to go in there somewhere, but after much deliberation I concluded that, for screen purposes, the best place was near the end. Just as you want to get the audience hooked from the start, so you need to keep them right through to the end and the postscript is a useful device. I also employed a number of flashbacks. In my opinion, du Maurier's best dialogue is reserved for her villains – Jack Favell and Rebecca. When Maxim remembers the blazing rows with Rebecca which culminated in her death, I wanted Rebecca to be seen – rather like a haunting portrait coming to life. And so on screen we hear her voice and see parts of her – her eyes, her lips, her hands. In addition, I changed the manner of her murder. In the book, Maxim shoots her, but I thought that was too

Rebecca (Lucy Cohu) taunts Maxim about her affairs and his precious Manderley.

cold, too premeditated. I felt that he acted out of sheer rage, pure jealousy, and that therefore the killing should be more tactile. So I had him strangle her, which seemed much more in keeping with the character and the sequence of events.'

Over the years, one of the chief areas of contention has been the depth and precise nature of the relationship between Rebecca and Mrs Danvers. Fearing censorship problems, the Hitchcock film played down the lesbian undertones, settling for a scene in Rebecca's bedroom where, in front of the new Mrs de Winter, Mrs Danvers tenderly caresses Rebecca's furs and underwear.

Arthur Hopcraft says: 'I have taken the sexuality between Rebecca and Mrs Danvers rather further than it has been done before. The language is very strong, in the way Mrs Danvers rails about the men in Rebecca's life, how she says that Rebecca used to come and tell her about them, to laugh about them. The implication to Mrs Danvers is clear – she thought she was the only one Rebecca loved. For Mrs Danvers, this was clearly a passionate affair (although we don't know whether it was reciprocated by Rebecca) and that is why she took her death so badly and ultimately became unhinged.'

> Fearing censorship problems, the Hitchcock film played down the lesbian undertones...

Jim O'Brien was suggested as director, and this was approved by Jonathan Powell. O'Brien, who had been widely praised for his outstanding work on *The Jewel in the Crown* and *The Monocled Mutineer*, had impressed Jonathan Powell with his direction of Carlton's *Beyond Reason* in 1995.

O'Brien, who sadly was taken ill towards the end of filming and had to be replaced for the final two and a half weeks of the ten-week schedule by Rob Knights, remembers: 'I had never read *Rebecca* before. But I was sent Arthur Hopcraft's script and I enjoyed it. Then I read the novel, and still liked the adaptation so I agreed to direct it. I could see what Arthur was doing. Above all, I wanted to make sure that the passion in the story came across, that it was not too dry and detached. In the book, Daphne du Maurier refers to passion in a very subtle, almost coded, manner. The whole story is told in a very understated way. A lot of girls read the story and they can treat it as being entirely innocent if they want to. But older women can see what du Maurier is getting at. I suppose this is part of the reason for the book's continuing success – that it appeals to people of all ages. We felt we needed to reflect this subtle passion on screen.'

One of O'Brien's first jobs was casting, although one of the principal artists was already in place – thanks to a chance meeting at a dinner two years previously.

Hilary Heath recalls: 'I was sitting next to Diana Rigg at a dinner. This was before I had even acquired the rights to *Rebecca* – I was just shouting my mouth off that I was hoping to do it! Diana looked at me and said: "I want to play Mrs Danvers." And I replied: "Right, you're on." Diana stood by us all the way – she was as good as her word. Obviously an actress of her calibre is in enormous demand but she actually turned down other things so that she could do *Rebecca*. She's been fantastic.'

'I was really excited about working with Diana,' enthuses Jim O'Brien. 'We had never worked together before but I had admired her work enormously. And it proved a thoroughly enjoyable experience. Diana was able to bring something fresh to the part of Mrs Danvers, a woman whom I feel was trapped by Rebecca's magic and actually became a victim of it herself, like Maxim. She is a very interesting character.'

The next to be cast was Charles Dance, who had worked with Jim O'Brien when he played Sergeant Guy Perron in *The Jewel in the Crown*, a performance which won Dance the BAFTA Best Actor award in 1984. Dance was the unanimous choice to play Maxim de Winter. 'If ever there was a part for somebody, this is Charlie's part,' enthuses Hilary Heath. 'He was very keen to do it and Maxim is one of the great, romantic parts. There's Heathcliff, Rochester and de Winter.'

Jim O'Brien agrees. 'Charles Dance was little known before *The Jewel in the Crown* but I've since become a great fan of his. He was certainly my first choice to play Maxim. He has brought many qualities to the role. I knew that he would be able to bring out the vulnerability, the compassion and the passion of the character. He has a large emotional range as an actor and has tremendous bearing. He is very convincing in that milieu. Of course, the difficulty is that Maxim has murdered his wife but whilst not necessarily making the character of Maxim wholly sympathetic, Arthur Hopcraft's adaptation does help us to understand why Maxim behaved the way he did.'

Casting director Doreen Jones adds: 'Naturally we wanted a star name to play Maxim and there are a limited number of big names, not only who are right for the part but who will do television. Charles Dance was the obvious choice. Besides being an excellent actor, he has all the physical attributes for Maxim – he's tall, broad-shouldered and good-looking.'

By far the biggest search was that conducted to find an actress to play the sec-

Charles Dance and Emilia Fox prepare for the next scene.

ond Mrs de Winter. 'Over a period of three days, I auditioned in the region of two hundred girls,' says Doreen Jones. 'Among the long shots was Emilia Fox, 21-year-old daughter of Edward Fox and Joanna David. Of course, Joanna had played the same part in the 1979 production of *Rebecca*. Millie was still at university but had played Colin Firth's younger sister in *Pride and Prejudice*. I eventually drew up a short list, which included her, but even then I considered her to be one of the rank outsiders. However she must have worked tremendously hard in the two weeks between our first meeting and the video reading because by the time we came to that, she was absolutely outstanding. Indeed my only reservation was that people might think we had picked her solely because of who her mother was, because it was a good publicity angle. Consequently, I deliberately didn't reveal Millie's family background to either Hilary Heath or Jim O'Brien in case they chose her for the wrong reasons.'

Hilary Heath confirms: 'I hadn't a clue that Millie was Joanna David's daughter. A lot of girls came up for the part, whom Doreen weeded out, and then quite a few came and read. They were all wonderful but it was clearly Millie's part. There was no contest – it was quite obvious that she was absolutely right for it. I think she is a real find.'

Jim O'Brien was equally enthusiastic. 'We could have cast with a more experienced and safer actress, but Millie seemed totally credible as a young woman of that age and that time. She has a terrific simplicity and is truly radiant on screen.'

For the role of Mrs Van Hopper, the producers wanted a Hollywood star. Hilary Heath used to be employed by International Creative Management (ICM), one of the world's leading theatrical agencies, and her work frequently took her to the United States. Through her contacts in the US, she knew Faye Dunaway's agent. She sent Dunaway the script for *Rebecca* and the actress was so impressed that she needed little persuading.

Doreen Jones admits that the producers also wanted a star name to play the villainous Jack Favell but in the end were won over by the audition of an up-and-coming actor, Jonathan Cake. 'I'd known Jonathan since he was at drama school,' says Doreen Jones, 'and I always knew he'd make it. He's spent years with the Royal Shakespeare Company and that experience shone through at the audition where he read so well that he convinced everybody that he was spot-on for the part. We were also delighted to get Geraldine James to play Maxim's sister, Beatrice. Like Charles Dance, she had worked with Jim O'Brien before in *The Jewel in the Crown*.

'I really do think we have assembled an excellent cast, right the way down to the more minor characters. Tom Chadbon, who plays Frank Crawley, is wonderful at playing good men without being too unctious. We were lucky to get Denis Lill to play such a small part as Beatrice's husband Giles and the same goes for Anthony Bate who plays Colonel Julyan. We even managed to land Timothy West as Dr Baker. At the time, Timothy was appearing in *Twelve Angry Men* at the Comedy Theatre but we arranged his one day's filming on *Rebecca* for a Sunday so he was able to do it on his day off.

'Dame Wendy Hiller was originally chosen to play Granny de Winter but sadly she was taken ill and Jean Anderson took over. At eighty-eight, Jean is a remarkable woman. She had been doing her own two-and-a-half hour one-woman show prior to this, so in comparison *Rebecca* was easy!

'I was also pleased to cast some local West Country actors in some of the smaller roles, such as the harbourmaster and the gardener, because it all helps with the

Opposite:
Emilia Fox as the
second Mrs de Winter.

authenticity of the accents.'

Potentially the most difficult role to cast was that of Rebecca herself. Even Daphne du Maurier doubted whether there were many actresses who could live up to her description of Rebecca, a woman of outstanding, striking beauty. 'Everyone who has read the book has their own image of Rebecca,' says Hilary Heath, 'and each image will probably be different. So we decided just to show glimpses of her, sometimes from the back, to create a suggestion of the character. That way, we would not destroy too many illusions.' Jim O'Brien adds: 'The story is about this perfect young woman, Rebecca. She is very much a mythical figure and therefore I just wanted to get a sense of her on screen. I didn't want her to be too human, partly because she only really existed in Daphne du Maurier's head.'

> 'Everyone who has read the book has their own image of Rebecca'

The actress chosen for the challenging role was Lucy Cohu, who is no stranger to period pieces, having appeared in a Catherine Cookson television adaptation. 'Lucy is very beautiful,' says Doreen Jones, 'and, to my mind, does live up to how the character would be. Furthermore, she has just the right voice for the part – confident and forthright. For viewers, she will make the character of Rebecca come alive.'

The new production has been watched with great interest by Daphne du Maurier's son, Christian Browning, who now lives at the old family home of Ferryside, overlooking Fowey harbour.

'Hilary Heath and I go back a long way,' says Browning. 'Her husband and I used to suffer together watching Chelsea Football Club! She asked me whether I would let her have first option when the US rights to *Rebecca* became available, which I was happy to do because I trusted her and knew her work. She and Robin Lowe came down and talked it over with me. Knowing the way television and, indeed, film works, I knew it was pointless making certain provisos – I just had to hope that they would stay as loyal to the original as possible. Having said that, you have to realise that the book has to be adapted. So much of my mother's writing was in her head and, of course, the whole of *Rebecca* was in the first person. This creates a problem for anyone wishing to adapt it, particularly as, for some reason, voice-overs seem to be frowned on these days even though one worked perfectly well in *Brideshead Revisited*.

'I think Arthur Hopcraft has done an excellent job and I am absolutely delighted with what I have seen so far. I made a fuss about a couple of things. I must admit at first I was vehemently against the character of Rebecca being seen on screen, but having heard how they were going to film her – with fleeting glimpses – I backed down and now I think it works really well. And our Rebecca looks absolutely stunning.

'When I received the first draft of Arthur's screenplay, I also objected to a passionate love scene towards the end where the second Mrs de Winter was described as 'straddling' Maxim in the bedroom. I wrote a big "NO" in the margin. The scene just jumped out of the page at me. I said that although Rebecca might have behaved like that, Mrs de Winter certainly wouldn't. The scene seemed completely wrong, particularly as it occurred just before they visited Dr Baker, a time when they would surely have had other things on their minds. I think Arthur wanted to inject a bit of spice but I knew my mother would not have approved. My sisters were equally horrified, so the scene was changed.

'My mother wrote love scenes in a very understated way. She left things for the reader's imagination and of course had to cater for her audience of the day. Arthur has done very well in highlighting the relationship between Rebecca and Mrs Danvers. To my mind, it was definitely a lesbian relationship, at least on Mrs Danvers' behalf, although it may not have actually been physical, perhaps more of a crush. For her part, Rebecca used Mrs Danvers to take her side and to provide her with an alibi when she was entertaining her men friends. I remember saying to my mother: "Surely Mrs Danvers is just a dyke." She would just laugh and remain non-committal, saying things like: "I didn't know what a dyke was until five years ago." My mother was a great tease. She was constantly playing games.'

Christian Browning was particularly impressed with the fine cast that had been assembled for the production. 'Emilia Fox is quite enchanting as Mrs de Winter. She is vulnerable to start with but gets progressively stronger, until in the end it is Maxim who has to lean on her. It is a wonderful performance. And it continues this amazing family link between the Foxes and the du Mauriers. Millie's great-aunt, Mary Fox, who went on that initial trip to discover Menabilly all those years ago, is still alive and lives in Lerryn in Cornwall, just a few miles from us. I remember Millie's father, Edward Fox, visiting Menabilly with his brother James. They were particularly friendly with my sisters. And their father Bob was great friends with my mother. Then, of course, Millie's mother, Joanna David, played Mrs de Winter in the BBC 1979 adaptation, and now it's Millie's turn. I know that if my mother could beam down to us, she would be absolutely delighted that Millie is playing her heroine.

'I also think that Charles Dance is extremely good as Maxim. It's a very

Timothy West as Dr Baker.

difficult role to cast. I don't know why, but people seem to imagine Maxim as dark-haired – perhaps it's the old cliché of tall, dark and handsome – and there is a reluctance to go for someone who is fair. But Charles is just right for the role. He plays it with enormous dignity and underplays it well. There is a tendency for actors playing Maxim to shout, but there is really no need. Maxim is a truly intriguing character. What fascinates me about the story as a whole is that we only ever have Maxim's version of what Rebecca was like. It was interesting that in Susan Hill's sequel *Mrs de Winter*, supposedly set ten years on, the question was posed as to whether Rebecca had really been that bad. We only have Maxim's word for it. Nobody else really had a bad word to say about her, apart from Ben. But then she had caught him peering through the cottage window while she was entertaining men so you could hardly blame her for being angry with him. Even Frank Crawley, when asked what Rebecca was like, had to admit that she was "the most beautiful creature I ever saw in my life." So Maxim is a multi-faceted character and Charles Dance has just the right expressions for him. He has that certain look.

'It almost goes without saying that I enjoyed Diana Rigg's interpretation of Mrs Danvers. And Faye Dunaway is wonderful as Mrs Van Hopper. She looks sensational and plays it crazy. And I think Jonathan Cake has done a fine job as Jack Favell, who should be a likeable villain. The problem facing anybody playing Favell is that George Sanders was the perfect smooth cad in the Hitchcock film. He's a tough act to follow. Whenever there is a stage tour of *Rebecca*, we tell whoever is playing Favell: "Go and see the film and just copy George Sanders." Sanders seems to have copyright on the part. Legend has it that when Sanders asked Hitchcock how he should play Favell, Hitchcock replied: "Just be yourself, George."

'On a more general note, I am pleased that there seems to be a revival in adapting the classics, particularly as it is something which British television has always done so well. I hope it will start a resurgence of interest in my mother's works, not that it has ever really waned, especially as Carlton have also bought her rather macabre short stories. They should open up a whole new audience to Daphne du Maurier – people who probably don't realise that it was she, and not Hitchcock, who wrote *The Birds*.'

The icily composed Mrs Danvers (Diana Rigg), is introduced to the second Mrs de Winter.

*The production team
prepare to create
Manderley at
Rotherfield Park in
Hampshire.*

CHAPTER FIVE

Manderley Revisited

While the actors were still being selected, the production team was also embarking on arguably the most important piece of casting of all – to find a suitable house to play Manderley. The house is a key element to the book, helping to create the mysterious, brooding atmosphere against which the heroine's life unfolds dramatically. To her, Manderley is an intimidating place, full of dark secrets and a shrine to her husband's seemingly omnipresent first wife. Finding the right building and the right location was absolutely essential to the success of the production and it was to prove a challenging task.

Daphne du Maurier left little room for manoeuvre. Her description of the house in the book is so vivid and detailed that to omit any facet would be likely to induce howls of protest from irate viewers. There are the wrought-iron gates and the lodge, the twisting, snaking drive through dense trees, the blood red rhododendrons, the sweeping staircase leading down to the hall, Rebecca's bedroom in the west wing, Rebecca's morning-room, the steep wooded hillside running down to the cove and finally the beach cottage itself. It soon became apparent that to find all of these requirements in one place would be a near-impossible task. After all, du Maurier herself had created Manderley from two separate houses – Menabilly and Milton.

One of the first places visited was Menabilly itself, if only to satisfy curiosity. But it was never under serious consideration to represent Manderley in its entirety. Hilary Heath explains: 'The Rashleigh family, who own Menabilly, wouldn't actually allow us to film there, but anyway it's not big enough. Manderley houses thirty servants and is a very large house, whereas Menabilly is just a country house.'

The search in earnest began in Ireland. 'I did a film in Ireland three years ago,' says Hilary Heath, 'called *An Awfully Big Adventure*, and for *Rebecca*, we looked at properties near Dublin. But a lot of the houses there are Victorian, whereas it states quite clearly in the book that Manderley has been in the family for three or four generations. Jim O'Brien is an absolute perfectionist so there was no question of using somewhere that was not built in the right period.'

Location manager Mark Mostyn joined the team in mid-February. With Ireland ruled out, the search switched to the West Country. 'We looked at something like thirty or forty houses in Devon and Cornwall,' recalls Mostyn, 'but it was very difficult to find anywhere which had the right exterior, the right interior plus the grounds. On a more practical basis, it also had to be somewhere we could film in for five or six weeks, somewhere which wasn't open to the public, and somewhere which was privately owned. We knew that wherever we chose, we would have to carry out a number of alterations to the house and you can only do that if it's privately owned. You couldn't do it to National Trust property. Similarly, it had to be a place where we could remove the existing furniture because wherever we went, we knew that we would have to redress the building, interior and exterior, to make it look like Manderley.'

From the outset, production designer Caroline Amies had a firm idea of what they were looking for. 'When I joined the production, my first job was to help find the house. I read the script, then I read the book before discussing with Jim O'Brien what sort of house it should be. What we wanted was somewhere which would work for the story and would also look good on screen. In the course of our search in Cornwall, we came across old photographs of a huge Jacobean house called The Coves which matched the description of Manderley in the book so perfectly that I feel Daphne du Maurier must have seen the place. It was set high on a wooded hill overlooking a cove near Helford – the area where du Maurier spent her honeymoon. It would probably have suited our purposes exactly but unfortunately it was demolished in the 1960s and has subsequently been replaced by a modern house.'

> ' ...you check it out first to make sure there is no undue noise...The last thing you want is jet aircraft rumbling overhead.'

Having met with little success in either Ireland or the West Country, the team began to concentrate their efforts closer to London. Caroline Amies explains: 'Our production base was established at Shepperton Studios to the south-west of London and it was decided that we should restrict our search for the house to somewhere within distance of the studios rather than have to take the crew away from base. This is perfectly understandable because you don't want to have to pay for crews to stay in hotels for weeks on end if you can avoid it. Producers want the money to be spent on the screen, not on hotels.'

After researching through books in libraries, a feasibility study was carried out on a succession of houses. Eventually a short-list of four possible houses was drawn up, at the top of which was Rotherfield Park, six miles south of Alton in Hampshire. Privately owned by Sir James Scott and standing in its own grounds, Rotherfield had already played host to a film crew, having been used as the venue for the Scottish wedding reception scene in *Four Weddings And a Funeral.*

'Rotherfield was ideal,' says Mark Mostyn. 'It is near enough to London but far enough away from main roads to be free of traffic noise. Also, it is not on any flight paths. Whenever you are contemplating using a particular location, you check it out first to make sure that there is not undue noise which is going to disrupt filming. This is particularly important with a period piece. The last thing you want is jet aircraft rumbling overhead. Sir James Scott was very keen on us using Rotherfield and was quite happy to put most of his furniture into storage for the duration of our stay.'

It took two weeks to get the house ready for filming. Various modern artifacts, such as television aerials, security lighting and a section of post-and-rail fencing, were all removed as the crew set about converting Rotherfield to Manderley.

Caroline Amies says: 'I discussed with the director who the de Winters were and how they lived to enable me to build up a picture of how the house should look. And then, rather than doing a glossy *Country Life* magazine, period interior, we did an eclectic interior, which is the sort of thing that happens when you've had generations living in the same house. I think the owners of Rotherfield decided that once they had made the commitment to allow us to film there, they'd let us get on with it. We completely redressed the interior with our own hired furniture and soft furnishings. We had curtains made and got the fabrics printed to our own design, something in keeping with what would be used by a wealthy country family in the Twenties. We also redecorated in a few places, but only to enhance the existing decorations. In fact, the owners liked our decorations so much that they kept them after we had finished filming.

'The staircase at Rotherfield is particularly impressive – I think that was what sold it to Jim O'Brien – and the house is full of fine paintings, many of which we were able to use. The only ones we didn't keep were those which were too modern.'

The painting which plays a vital part in the plot is that of Lady Caroline de Winter, the lady in white, a copy of whose dress the heroine wears with such disastrous effect to the fancy dress ball. Caroline Amies reveals: 'Our painting of the lady in white was based on a Gainsborough, although it's not actually a white dress in the Gainsborough, and we also made her look a little more enigmatic. I phoned artist Jane Gifford, with whom I'd worked on the film *Carrington*, and asked: "How's your Gainsborough, Jane?" I gave her the reference and the sizes and she painted it in the style of Gainsborough in three weeks. We actually got her to do the painting to the size of the frame that was available, rather than the other way round. You don't want to construct a new frame to fit the painting, because it will always look new. What you want, and what we have been able to use, is a very good quality period frame.'

Outside, the herbaceous borders were planted up and the building itself was softened with creepers where necessary. However, in spite of its many virtues, Rotherfield was by no means the answer to all of the crew's dreams and it was apparent that more than one location would be needed to recreate Manderley. For although the view of the house from the drive at Rotherfield was very good, as were the interior and exterior, the house itself was deemed too small. To give the impression of a much larger house, it was decided to use optical effects to 'mount on' the wings of a second house, Montacute, near Yeovil. By shooting both houses in identical lighting conditions and resorting to technical trickery, it was possible to create an image of the two buildings combined. Thus Rotherfield suddenly acquired a west wing from another county and the exterior of Manderley became a combination of Rotherfield Park and Montacute House.

'We ended up with a compromise,' says Caroline Amies, 'to get an interior which worked in some aspects. Rotherfield is not old enough to indicate that it has been lived in for three hundred years (as had Manderley) so what we have tried to suggest is that there is a Jacobean palace, part of which is still standing, with an early Victorian pile stuck on to it. To this end, we used a wing of Montacute House which is probably one of the most beautiful Jacobean palaces in Britain. This played the west wing of Manderley, although the interiors of the west wing were built on the stage at Shepperton.'

In fact, another house was used for some of the interiors of Manderley – Nether Winchendon, near Aylesbury. Caroline Amies explains: 'In the book, Rebecca's morning-room and beach cottage interior were very much hers. They carried her trademark and, as such, were much more sensual. Although Rotherfield has a separate drawing-room, we wanted something which looked special, something which had a different feel to it. We wanted to push towards the Jacobean which is more sensual, rather than Victorian which is a bit lumpy and heavy.' The drawing-room at Nether Winchendon proved ideal. A second day's filming also took place there as the exterior was considered just right for Granny de Winter's house.

Jim O'Brien says: 'There simply wasn't one house which suited all our needs for Manderley. The atmosphere of the main rooms at Rotherfield was perfect. They had a tremendous weight and seriousness. A lot of the houses we looked at were too light and airy and just not grand enough. So at Rotherfield we filmed in the main hall, the staircase, the dining-room and the library. But we needed somewhere else for Rebecca's morning-room and we had to recreate her bedroom in the studio.'

Having found the houses to represent Manderley, the next problem was finding somewhere which had the necessary requirements for the grounds, since the drive at Rotherfield was unsuitable. Again, there were geographical restrictions on the search.

'We had to fit in geographically with what was being shot on certain days,' says Caroline Amies. 'We might have found the perfect drive in northern Scotland but that was no good to us when we were filming in the south of England. As it was, the drive, like the house, was a composite affair. The lodge had to match up with the sandstone of Rotherfield. We couldn't use any old lodge – it had to hold the architectural feel. In the end, we managed to find a good lodge and a nice set of iron gates at Mentmore in Buckinghamshire, so we got permission to film there.'

Alas, the rest of the drive at Mentmore failed to match the description in the book and there were no rhododendrons. For the real nightmare for the production team surrounded the blood-red rhododendrons. As Rotherfield is on a chalk soil, the flowers will not grow there, and so the quest began to find a twisting, wooded drive lined with red rhododendrons. A Hertfordshire house called Champneys fulfilled part of the criteria. It had a twisting back drive and plenty of rhododendrons. Unfortunately, they were purple, not red.

'We searched high and low but nowhere could we find a mass of big red rhododendrons,' laments Caroline Amies. 'Eventually, we decided to go with the purple ones. Jim O'Brien liked the colour, which is very powerful. So we filmed at Champneys and planted purple rhododendrons along part of the drive at Rotherfield to match up. We had to bring our filming schedule forward a bit so that we could catch them in full bloom. But by the time we came to shoot the interiors of Rebecca's rooms, they had all finished flowering, so for cut flowers in the house, we used bright red peonies instead. It really was a headache. I never want to hear about another blooming rhododendron as long as I live...'

Thus, like the second Mrs de Winter, the viewer will be taken on an eventful journey on first approaching Manderley. For the road leading up to the gates was shot in Devon; the gates and lodge were at Mentmore; the rhododendron drive was at Champneys; another section of wooded drive was shot in Devon, and all leading to a house, parts of which are in Hampshire, Somerset and Buckinghamshire. Thanks to the magic of television, nobody will be able to spot the joins.

There would also have to be another cutting-off point, for none of the properties are anywhere near the sea and the description of Manderley is that it stands on a wooded hill which leads down to a cove and a beach. Mark Mostyn says: 'We knew that we would see the characters leaving the woods at Rotherfield and pick them up through the woods down to the cove. It was surprisingly difficult to find woods that come right down to coves, so that you can walk out of woods, on to the beach and into the sea. Initially, before we went down to Cornwall to search for

The second Mrs de Winter makes her entrance at the fancy dress ball as Lady Caroline de Winter.

Frith (John Horsley) and the other domestic staff and estate workers assemble to welcome Maxim and his new bride to Manderley.

somewhere suitable, we thought about getting a helicopter to recce the whole of the coastline. Eventually, we got out all of the Ordnance Survey maps of the area but found very few places where woods went right down to a cove. It took myself and unit manager John Bamford a week to check out all of the wooded coves in Cornwall and we then stretched into Devon, up as far as Lyme Regis. What made it more complicated was that the woodland had to be steep-sided. We tended to find wooded areas around river estuaries which meant that straight ahead, instead of the view out to sea which we wanted, you just had the other side of the estuary. And that destroyed everything, because the view had to look right out to sea for the shipwrecking scene where the freighter goes aground and the divers haul up Rebecca's yacht.

'We did think about using the cove near Helford where the old house had been but we decided that the cove at Mothecombe on the Fleet estate was better. It's a very beautiful spot, just in Devon between Kingsbridge and Plymouth. Another advantage is that the beach at Mothecombe is private so we didn't have to worry about tourists who can be a problem for film-makers in the West Country in summer. It also overlooks a stretch of water which is rarely used by boats or windsurfers, so again that was fortunate.

The only thing Mothecombe lacked was the beach cottage where Rebecca entertained her men friends. The solution was simple – the construction department built their own.

Caroline Amies explains: 'We constructed the exterior on the beach at Mothecombe and did the interiors in the studio at Shepperton. As with the lodge, the cottage had to blend in architecturally with the house at Rotherfield. It had to be believable that it was part of the same estate. The cottage was made from timber and plaster. It was partly prefabricated but it was basically built on the site over a period

of two weeks. When we had finished filming, it was demolished and thrown on a skip.'

    A separate location was required for the scene where Maxim is seen sinking Rebecca's yacht in the dead of night. Mark Mostyn says: 'We needed a pier which went out to sea and which we could film from and put lights on. This was so that we could shoot Rebecca's yacht out at sea with nothing on the horizon behind, because the yacht was supposed to be some distance out. We looked at all the piers and harbours on the South Cornwall coast and settled upon Charlestown, near St Austell. Like Mothecombe, it happens to be privately owned so, from my point of view, it was easy to control. Whenever you're filming in somewhere like Devon or Cornwall, you're always thinking how you're going to be able to service those locations. For *Rebecca*, it was essential that we chose somewhere with good road access because wherever we went, we had a crew of between sixty and seventy and our vehicles consisted of twenty large trucks, winnebagos, mobile homes, dining buses, the lot. It was like the circus coming to town.

    'For Charlestown, the need for access was even more important because we had huge cranes to lift the yacht in and out of the water as well as a 'cherry-picker', which is a 100 ft-high elevated platform, on which we put lights. We put the cherry-picker, which was brought to Charlestown by lorry, on the end of the pier to backlight the scene of the yacht being sunk. The backlight looks like moonlight and also gives a nice reflection on the sea.'

    The decision to film Manderley mostly in Hampshire has not met with the wholesale approval of the people of Cornwall, who regard Daphne du Maurier as one of their own and insist that *Rebecca* should have been filmed there. A number of national newspapers carried the views of Malcolm Brown, a member of Restormel Borough Council, St Austell, who voiced his disapproval of the choice of venue. 'The story is set in Cornwall,' he declared, 'and the actual house is often

Maxim de Winter and the second Mrs de Winter arrive at Manderley.

thought to be based on du Maurier's own home at Menabilly. Menabilly is the one property most closely associated with du Maurier and I feel that filming in Hampshire is unwise when there are so many opportunities in Cornwall with its dramatic coastline. The people of Cornwall are aggrieved. From a tourism point of view, there is no doubt that it would have encouraged people to come here and see where the film was set.'

Rebecca producer Hilary Heath admits: 'We've come in for a lot of flak from the people of Cornwall, but we have actually done a fair bit of filming down there. The really difficult location to find was the trees coming down to the water's edge – had we found it in Cornwall, we would have gone there. As for the house, Rotherfield Park is in Hampshire and, contrary to popular opinion, it was in Hampshire, at Greyfriars near Fleet, where Daphne du Maurier wrote the vast majority of the book.'

> Unfortunately, boats were to prove as big a headache as rhododendrons.

Furthermore, it should be remembered that whilst *Rebecca* is undeniably set in Cornwall, Manderley is by no means based solely on Menabilly, with Milton House in Northamptonshire also having a claim to fame.

Christian Browning, Daphne du Maurier's son, points out that some of the locations which inspired his mother are not practical for television. 'Menabilly is simply not big enough to play Manderley,' he says, 'and Pridmouth Bay is inaccessible to a large television crew – what I call the last of the travelling circuses. When Hilary Heath and Arthur Hopcraft first came to see me, I took them to Pridmouth to give them a taste of the atmosphere. Unfortunately, it was a cloudy day and, to be honest, Pridmouth Bay didn't look all that good. It was a bit dirty and covered in seaweed. Mothecombe, where they eventually filmed, is much nicer. But the trouble is local councillors and so on sometimes allow their hearts to rule their heads. They simply don't appreciate the mechanics of filming. Of course it would have been nice to film Manderley in Cornwall, but at least this production is not being shot in California like the Hitchcock movie. And I guarantee that when the people of Canada and New Zealand see it on television, they'll have absolutely no idea that it wasn't filmed in Cornwall.'

'We were very happy with Rotherfield Park,' adds Caroline Amies, 'and everyone there was incredibly helpful. It can be a lot to put up with when you have all of the crew and the trucks rolling up at 6.30am for three weeks. Obviously, we did our best to keep any disruption to a minimum because you're aware when you go filming that if you don't treat these locations with delicacy and respect, you'll ruin it not only for yourself, but for other film companies. You simply won't get invited back again.'

Indeed the only note of discord surrounded Rotherfield Park's resident labrador, Flossie, who began putting on weight at an alarming rate after dining on daily titbits from the crew. An edict had to go out on the crew's daily call sheet urging them to refrain from feeding the dog. It read: 'Please note that Flossie the house dog is putting on vast amounts of weight and is close to exploding. Although it is very hard not to give in to her begging, please could everyone stop feeding her. She was originally a small labrador without coronary problems!'

Unfortunately, boats were to prove as big a headache as rhododendrons. It all started promisingly enough. Mark Mostyn contacted boat expert Tony Tucker and, after receiving the brief, Tucker found a suitable vessel sitting in a back garden in Devon, surrounded by nettles. Art director Frank Walsh takes up the story: 'The yacht Tony found was perfect for the period but it had lost a lot of its varnish. Anyway it was dug out from this patch of weeds and we could see that it was just right for the end shot of Rebecca's yacht being resurrected from the deep. So we decided to film it out of order chronologically, doing the shots where we pulled it up from the sea before we did those of it actually being sunk. We had to do a bit of work on it first, putting in things like portholes, and then it was taken to Charlestown Harbour for the shot of it being lifted out of the water by crane. We dressed it up with seaweed and sand to make it look as if it had been at the bottom of the sea for a year. But of course before we could haul it up, we ourselves had to sink it. From the state of the boat, which was nothing more than a holey bucket, you would have thought it would have gone under straight away. The whole of the bottom of the boat had rotted away. But in spite of its dilapidated condition, it steadfastly refused to sink. We ended up having to fill it with ballast and Tony had to insert sea-cocks. Then a diver released the cocks to allow the boat to fill up with water and finally down she went.

'After those shots had been completed, the boat was taken on a trailer to a boatyard in Salcombe where it was repaired and made seaworthy. It was generally smartened up. It was given a new canvas, the bits of broken timber were replaced and then the varnish wood effect was recreated. The end result was a pretty yacht for Rebecca.

'Having restored the boat, we were ready to do the shots where Maxim sunk it. These were scheduled to take place at a night shoot at Charlestown in mid-August. Originally we were just going to sink the yacht down to its cabin but it was then decided that the boat should be sunk right under the water so that it disappeared completely from view. Consequently, there was a fair amount of last-minute re-jigging, and shooting the scene took much longer than we had previously anticipated. The boat was taken out to sea as planned but the filming chances meant that we would have to keep an eye on the tide. We knew that the tide would be out around 3.30am so we knew we'd be up against it. And sure enough the tide went out, not only faster than we could get the shots done but also before we could haul the boat safely ashore. The boat ended up fouling on rocks beneath the water and by the time we had finally managed to get it out of the water, we'd lost the tide. There was a fair amount of damage to the boat and we had to bring it back to the harbour by crane.

'There had to be a quick re-think of the shots required and the final sequence of tight shots of Charles Dance on the boat were actually done on the beach, on dry land. To create the effect of a rain-lashed, windswept night at sea, we brought in the rain and wind machines which we had on standby and got half a dozen members of the production crew to rock the boat back and forth! Earlier the weather had been very kind to us, giving us the rough sea we wanted, so now we had to match conditions up with the previous shots. Whilst the rough seas were great for us, I'm not sure that Charles Dance would agree. I don't think he was too keen on having to go out there – in the end he was probably quite relieved to do it on dry land. I think we were glad to see the back of that boat. First it wouldn't sink for us and then it wouldn't come up!

'Another boat which caused us a problem or two was the stricken freighter which we wanted to film going aground at Mothecombe. We only had a choice of about four ships that were available. Our first choice was a working vessel. It was

Maxim de Winter awaits the arrival of his new love.

based in Plymouth but was often away carrying out deep sea surveys and we knew it would be tricky to fit its commitments into our schedule. And the week when we needed it, the ship was up in the Irish Sea, rendering it unavailable. So we turned to our second choice – a three-masted schooner which was being used off the Isle of Wight as part of Cowes Week. But on the Sunday, the day we wanted it to sail back to Devon, it was rammed off Cowes, fouling its propellor and making it unseaworthy. So we had to make a series of frantic calls, going on bended knee, pleading to get our original choice back from the Irish Sea in time. We knew that our last available day in Devon was on the Friday and mercifully it arrived on the Thursday night. All in all, it was a close-run thing.

'Once we'd got the boat, we set about dressing it for the part. We extended the funnel and concealed the various items of surveying apparatus which were spread all over the deck, because the freighter in the story would not have had such equipment. By positioning anchors off the side of the vessel, we were able to rig it off the rocks as if it was listing. To add to the atmosphere, we managed to obtain period lifeboats and small craft from the Plymouth area.'

*Opposite:
The girl appears,
delighted to see
Maxim.*

But even then, as location manager Mark Mostyn reveals, there was nearly a calamitous outcome. 'On the Friday morning, we arrived at Mothecombe to be greeted by a thick fog. We'd done all the scenes looking the other way two days earlier in brilliant sunshine so we needed to match them up. We had no spare days so

we were praying that the fog would lift in time. Luckily, this time the Gods were smiling on us and the fog did indeed lift.'

Apart from Hampshire and the West Country, the other principal location was the south of France for the scenes where Maxim conducts his whirlwind courtship of the heroine. 'We filmed on the Côte d'Azur around Monte Carlo,' says Caroline Amies, 'using a predominantly French crew. The main thing when you go there is that you want to say: "This is the south of France." Otherwise there is no point in going all that way – we might as well have stayed in England. So the director made sure he got plenty of landscape shots to show off the scenery and to let the viewer know that we really had gone to France and not filmed those scenes in Dorset or somewhere else.'

The expedition to the south of France was blighted by appalling weather – two days of torrential thunderstorms and another half-day of bad weather which was, to say the least, unfortunate for that region in August. Ironically, some of the scenes had to be picked up in Cornwall the following week where the weather was excellent!

Dr Baker breaks the news to Jack Favell (Jonathan Cake), Col. Julyan (Anthony Bate), the second Mrs de Winter and her husband Maxim, that Rebecca had been suffering from cancer.

The interiors for the French hotel were filmed at Luton Hoo in Bedfordshire. The exteriors in France were found at approximately the same time as Luton Hoo which meant that they could be nicely matched up. Caroline Amies says: 'We were looking for a Ritz-style hotel and Luton Hoo is one of the few houses in the country with a suitable interior. It is ideal because the house hasn't been modernised. Also, it stands in its own grounds and is relatively isolated, which was a great advantage. If you've got the perfect period location but it has something like a pylon nearby, you can still go ahead with filming – such have been the technical advancements that, at a cost, you can remove things like pylons in post production.

But it's still preferable if you can find somewhere like Luton Hoo where you don't have to worry about those things. We filmed in four of the bedrooms and embellished the walls with our own wallpaper. We also had to bring in all our hired furniture.

'If we need something particular that we can't get, we either buy it or get one of the hire companies to buy it on our behalf. Rebecca's bed in her west-wing bedroom proved tricky. It was difficult finding something that was sumptuous enough. We ended up hiring a bed which we then copied, increased in size and turned into a four-poster. The result was a bed 7ft by 7ft by 12ft high. After shooting, we sold it back to the hire company.

'The other item which was awkward to find was the china cupid which the heroine accidentally smashes. You'd think it would be easy to find a china cupid but whilst we came up with lots of cherubs, there were no cupids. After a long search, we eventually got something from Italy but even then it wasn't a cupid and had to be altered by the makers in three weeks to turn the arm so that they could put in the bow and arrow. We had a total of six made in case we needed to do a number of takes. They were scored beforehand to make sure they actually smashed instead of just bouncing, so we had some sort of control. Funnily enough, we heard afterwards that in order to remedy a gap in the market which we had drawn to their attention, the Italian firm are now planning to produce china cupids.'

> '**You'd think it would be easy to find a china cupid but whilst we came up with lots of cherubs, there were no cupids.**'

Other locations were found in and around London. The scenes in Dr Baker's consulting room were filmed at the law courts at Inner and Middle Temple; the coroner's court scenes were shot at a disused magistrates' court at Stratford East; and the bar of the luxury liner bringing Maxim and his new bride back to England was recreated at a Brixton rock venue! Mark Mostyn recalls: 'We were looking for a 1920s Art Deco-style bar and such things are not easy to find. We studied real liners but couldn't find anything that hadn't been modernised or was the right style. Flicking through a book, I saw pictures of Brixton Academy, an arts and music venue. The style of the bar there was exactly what we wanted and so we filmed there. To recreate the liner bobbing up and down on the sea, we used a moving camera. The other interiors on the liner were all shot at Shepperton.'

In terms of visual impact, the most spectacular scene in *Rebecca* is probably the fire. This was staged partly at Rotherfield Park (for exterior shots) and partly in the studio at Shepperton (for the interiors). Understandably, home owners become a shade anxious when they hear that their house is going to be set on fire and Sir James Scott at Rotherfield was no exception until it was explained to him that the towering inferno would be a trick of special effects without a single flame and would therefore be perfectly safe.

The great fire of Manderley was staged by special effects expert Joss Williams. 'I decided to use flares rather than propane gas jets because flares are more controllable and more cost-effective than flame. There is an element of risk with all special effects but, in the case of fires, that risk is greatly reduced when you don't have to deal with real flames. The other advantage is that flares are quicker to re-set should you need to do more than one take. For the long and mid-shots, I wanted to recreate something like the Blitz, with an orange glow lighting up the night sky.

Maxim informs Mrs Danvers that it was his wife who broke the china cupid, not the footman, Robert.

I put one flare (of 100,000 candles power) up on the roof of Rotherfield and placed four incidental smoke machines at ground level. The flare was ignited electrically by one of our men on the roof and there was also a firefighter up there for safety purposes just in case things went wrong. I'm pleased to say it worked first time. There was a good orange glow and plenty of smoke – it looked just like the real thing. And the fact of the matter is we didn't need flames because when a building is burning out of control, you rarely see any from the outside. In a real fire, the roof usually falls through and the flames are sucked back in, either through the roof or the windows.

'We needed three interior shots of the fire – one in Rebecca's bedroom, one in the upstairs corridor and one on the great staircase. Obviously, we couldn't do those scenes at Rotherfield so we filmed them in the studio with stunt doubles for Diana Rigg and Charles Dance. I had the sets constructed from non-combustible materials like timber and plaster and I used propane to create the flames and either paraffin wad or controllable alcohol to spread them along the set. The whole fire was superficial. None of the set was burnt at all. If it burns, it means I haven't done my job. One of the things you have to make sure you avoid when creating fires is black smoke. Not only is it highly dangerous but it completely wrecks the shot. No camera can see through it.'

Opposite: Manderley ablaze, a triumph of special effects.

The other big special effect in *Rebecca* is the firework display at the fancy

dress ball. This too was filmed at Rotherfield. 'We bought the fireworks from a supplier,' says Joss Williams, 'and we used about a hundred in all, arranging them in small groups on the ground. It was very much a ground display — there was nothing higher than 15ft in the air. We had to make sure that the fireworks were of the sort that would have been seen in the Twenties. Although coloured fireworks had been introduced in the 1890s, the director was keen to go with just silver and gold. They look classy. Again, everything went smoothly. There should never be a danger with special effects if things are planned properly, but you have to realise what you're dealing with and observe caution at all times. In fact, the biggest danger is people getting too blasé. And sadly that's when things can go wrong.'

The spectacular fireworks display in the grounds of Manderley.

*Opposite:
Servants, estate workers and firemen try to put out the blaze.*

Chapter Six

Dressing for the Part

The world was changing rapidly in the mid-Twenties. It was an era that heralded the arrival of birth control clinics, radio and jazz; that saw the emergence of influential figures such as Agatha Christie, P G Wodehouse and Coco Chanel; when the craze was for the upper-classes to dance the night away to the tango or the charleston while the working classes watched as unemployment topped one million, leading to widespread discontent and Britain's first general strike in 1926.

It was a time when women were asserting their independence in the clothes they wore and the things they did. There was widespread concern as skirts were seen to rise and morals decline in unison. The style was for a flat chest, straight clothes and short hair as women, many of whom had done men's jobs during the First World War, decided that they wanted styles to reflect their new-found freedom. If they could do the work of men, why couldn't they dress like men too? Guardians of old-fashioned values voiced their disapproval of the new fashions, fearing that they would encourage loose behaviour, particularly when combined with other disturbing new trends among women such as smoking, drinking alcohol and wearing make-up. It reached the point where women caught with short skirts and bare arms in Chicago were liable to a $100 fine. Catholic bishops in Italy banned scantily clad or bare-legged women from church while in Great Britain, doctors warned that the prevailing fashions might be bad for the wearer's health, causing puffiness and chafing of the legs — something which had rarely been a problem with long skirts. In February 1926, British medical experts condemned the craze for women who wanted to look like 'weak and weedy men', suggesting that the quest for a willowy figure could increase the risk of consumption. All in all, it was a turbulent time on the fashion front.

The task of dressing *Rebecca* fell to costume designer Liz Waller, herself no stranger to the requirements of period drama. In addition to winning an Emmy Award for *Elizabeth R* (starring Glenda Jackson) and a BAFTA for Best Costume Design for *The Camomile Lawn*, Liz had recreated the Twenties look in series such as *Agatha Christie's Poirot* and *Reilly — Ace of Spies*.

'When I received the script for *Rebecca*, the first thing I did was go through it and break it down into what I thought I needed costume-wise. Then I discussed it

> Guardians of old-fashioned values voiced their disapproval of the new fashions, fearing that they would encourage loose behaviour...

A relaxing moment in-between takes.

with the director. In the meantime, I was collecting my reference, which came mostly from original photographs of people of a similar class to the characters in *Rebecca* and in similar situations. We found plenty of good pictorial reference about the Twenties which gave us a very good idea of what people of that class wore.

'Once I had got that vision in my mind and once we had worked out which seasons of the year the scenes were supposed to be set in, we went to the costumier and looked at everything that was hanging on the rails. Where possible, I tried to use real clothes from the Twenties because there are still quite a lot around, but obviously if they are not in good enough condition, you have to have them made. The costumier I got most of the clothes from was Cosprop in London. They're very helpful and sympathetic. If you say you want a dress miserable and dowdy, they make it miserable and dowdy, whereas lots of costumiers won't do that — they want their stuff to look showy on screen.

'What I like to do is take the actor in, gather everything from the costumier's rail, get the actor to try it on and work out what looks good on them proportionally. You can have an idea of how you want somebody to look but it may not be right for their body. So I like actors to try on a lot of real clothes so that I can get a feeling for what the best shapes of the period are for them. Depending on what is available, we then had to mix the real clothes with those we had specially made. When we had clothes made, we tried to use the genuine fabrics of the period or, if the condition of those fabrics was poor, we attempted to find a modern fabric that equated with the original quality. The cut of Twenties clothes is so simple and it works, but if you try to be clever and modern with them, they don't work. I think people tend to put too much detail on to Twenties clothes. Some modern buttons will fit perfectly into the Twenties style and be undetectable but others you simply can't use because everybody will recognise them for what they are.

> 'In the Thirties, nobody would bat an eyelid at a woman wearing trousers but in the Twenties, Rebecca wouldn't have worn trousers unless they were men's.'

'One of the potential pitfalls on *Rebecca* is that the book was written in 1938 but was largely set around 1926. Taking the ill-fitting jumper which the second Mrs de Winter was said to wear in her youth, there's a big difference between an ill-fitting jumper of 1938 and one from 1926. A 1938 jumper is not unattractive but a 1926 one is hideous. So we had to make allowances for the difference in period. In the book, Rebecca is described as wearing trousers. In the Thirties nobody would bat an eyelid at a woman wearing trousers but in the Twenties, Rebecca wouldn't have worn trousers unless they were men's trousers. That was tricky for us, because trousers for women didn't really come in until 1931. We did end up putting her in trousers but we had to be very careful about the style so that it was authentic.

'The Twenties are an incredibly difficult period to wear. We were lucky in that Emilia Fox is a perfect shape for it because she's got a lovely, long slim neck, nice straight shoulders and she's not too curvaceous. You can get an actress with a bosom and they look lovely in Thirties clothes but not so good in Twenties fashions. That's the thing about Twenties clothes — they hang from the bosom. We had a three-hour fitting session with Millie where we tried a lot of different shapes to see what suited her best. Everybody tends to think that *Rebecca* is a great romantic piece and that therefore the heroine, the second Mrs de Winter, has to look lovely, but from the book it is quite clear that she wasn't fashionable at all. She does have to look attractive, but in a wholesome way. She mustn't be showy and flamboyant like Rebecca herself.

'Characterisation is very important. It is essential that you dress the production so that the clothes look real on that person — they must suit the shape of the actor. Reality is the keynote. *Rebecca* is quite a dowdy piece in a funny way but you have to make it look attractive. But there is a big difference between attractive and glamorous.

'Most of Emilia's outfits had to be made up — suits, coats and dresses — because a lot of the clothes we liked weren't in particularly good condition. We used the original clothes as a template and then copied them. For the white dress which she wore to the fancy dress ball as Lady Caroline de Winter, we interpreted the painting which had been chosen by the designer and the director. We made it eighteenth-century but we cheated a bit by fastening it down the front. We boned the bodice rather than putting the dress on over a corset simply because Millie has to put it on in shot and it was easier for her to do it that way.

'Diana Rigg and I talked at length about Mrs Danvers and how she should look. Diana wanted her to look rather old-fashioned so her clothes are from a different era — just after the First World War. Diana wanted Mrs Danvers to wear only dark clothes, which matches the description of the character in the book. She had two dresses because, being a housekeeper in a large house, she would have some sort of uniform. We had one navy blue dress with a lace collar made for the day and then for evening she just had a plain black silk dress. We had to get some light into the black dress to stop it looking like a big black blob on screen so we chose a texture with a pattern on it which showed up nicely when the light hit it. Most of Diana's clothes had to be made but we did manage to find a real hat and a coat.'

Arthur Hopcraft's adaptation has made Mrs Van Hopper, the heroine's vulgar American employer, slightly more glamorous than Daphne du Maurier's original creation and her wardrobe had to be tailored accordingly. 'Faye Dunaway was extremely happy that Mrs Van Hopper was a bit more glamorous and a lot less gaudy than in the book,' says Liz Waller. 'So the character didn't have to be a monument to bad taste. I bought quite a lot of real clothes for Faye. In particular, she likes wearing real underwear and negligées and I had everything copied so that we had two lots of it. She had three dresses, all of which were also the genuine article although we did have to doctor two of them in places. For example, her orange chiffon dress had to be refurbished because it was falling away in places and for her lace dress, we made a new slip to go underneath it. Mrs Van Hopper was usually bedecked with jewellery and we managed to fit her with real period pieces in jade and diamanté.

'All of Charles Dance's clothes had to be made because he is such a big man. Nothing "off the peg" would fit him and so we had the wardrobe of an English country gentleman made specially for him. Such clothes don't come cheap, with the result that a third of the costume budget for the show went on Charles. Each suit cost in the region of £1,500, his shoes were £100 a pair and his shirts worked out at £90 apiece. Shirts, in particular, have to be duplicated so that one can be in the wash. You can't rely on just having the one, not only in case of accidents but also because, if you're working late, you can't get it washed and dried in time for the next day's shoot. One thing we were able to buy for Charles was his hat, but even that had to be adapted because the brim was too wide for him. So wardrobe supervisor Colin Lavers cut round it very carefully to trim off the unwanted material and reduce the brim.

'I am pleased to say that nothing has really defeated us on *Rebecca*. True, it was almost impossible to find seamed stockings from the period but we got around that by buying a plain pair and then sewing a seam up the back.'

The biggest single day in terms of numbers, and therefore potentially the most hazardous for the wardrobe department, was the fancy dress ball, filmed at Rotherfield in June. While the props department were required to produce such items as a barrel of cider, a string of fairy lights, huge flower arrangements, instruments for the band plus assorted cutlery, glasses, plates, tables and chairs, wardrobe and make-up had to contend with a dozen speaking actors plus 120 extras — 50 dancing guests, 50 drinking guests, six band members, five footmen, four estate workers, two kitchen maids, one cook, one vegetable cook and one housemaid.

> 'Each suit cost in the region of £1,500, his shoes were £100 a pair and his shirts worked out at £90 apiece.'

Liz Waller says: 'We tried to assemble clothes which the Cornish gentry of the time would genuinely have worn to a fancy dress ball and not make it look like a fancy dress ball which had come from a costume house. For example, Beatrice's husband, Giles, was supposed to be an Arab sheikh. Denis Lill, who plays Giles, thought it would be funny if he wore his evening dress underneath the costume. So he wore a bow tie and stiff shirt with the Arab robes on top, but with the bow tie still sticking out, because that was something which Giles himself would probably have done. Similarly, Beatrice's clothes were something she'd have made up from the dressing-up box. She was supposed to be the Queen of the Desert and wore a pea-green chiffon dress with lots of coins dangling. It was a very noisy costume...

'Frank Crawley went as a pirate, so we made that up with big boots and a big hat. And we cut out a skull and crossbones to make it look as if he hadn't gone to a costumier but had actually rustled up something himself.

'Some of the more historical costumes were hired, such as Napoleon, but that was given a nice touch by the fact that he was wearing his First World War medals. We had a few eighteenth-century costumes with a Twenties slant.

'The ball was fun but also extremely hard work. We started at 7am to get the actors ready for 10am on set and we didn't finish until half past midnight the following morning. And there were only the six of us looking after 120 complex costumes. As far as possible, everything was organised beforehand. Each of the walk-on artists had their own coathangers and their own chair with their name on, so they knew where to go. And we had a big marquee set up in the grounds of Rotherfield as an extra dressing-room. Luckily, the weather held — if it had been raining, it would have been a nightmare. The extras did get a bit hot but the only accidents were the usual problem of coffee being spilt down the front of white dress shirts.'

The consultant on *Rebecca* is Robin Lowe, the consultant for the du Maurier estate. 'I was originally going to be called technical adviser,' says Lowe, 'but I thought that made it sound as if I changed the light bulbs on set! My role on the production has been to see that the spirit of the book is carried out on screen and I must say I think Arthur Hopcraft's adaptation is very loyal.

'Also, I have the advantage of being the only person connected with the production who was actually around in the Twenties when the bulk of the story was set. True, I was less than two years old at the time but I can remember how things were around that period. What I have tried to do is keep an eye open for detail — the little things which may seem insignificant to some people but which need to be done correctly to ensure that the piece is wholly authentic. So from time to time, I would quietly make suggestions that things could be said or done slightly differently. Most of the time, my ideas were taken on board. Occasionally, usually because it was too late, they were unable to incorporate my thoughts.

'For example, nobody ever shook hands in those days — the form of greeting was much stiffer, more formal and purely verbal. So I pointed that out. Also, from my recollection of the customs of the time, I knew that housemaids always changed their uniform in the afternoon. Again, it's a small point but it's best to get these things right and everyone on *Rebecca* was keen to do just that. Then somebody raised the question of whether a butler knocked at the door before entering. I was able to say that he did but after knocking, he would walk straight in. I also picked up the odd anachronism — words that weren't quite right. For example, nobody said "scotch" in those days. It was "whisky" because there was no choice then.

'I also had discussions with the costume designer about some of the clothing, suggesting that the men's ties should be regimental and club ties rather than spotted because that was what was worn in the country prior to the Second World War. I suppose my only reservation is that there are too many plain white shirts worn by the men. In those days, country folk mostly wore striped flannel shirts. But you can't win everything.'

Producer Hilary Heath pays tribute to Robin Lowe's contribution. 'He moved in those circles at the time and has been very helpful. And as he would tell me when he wanted to make a point: "At least I was alive then, darling!"'

Just as the characters in *Rebecca* have to be dressed according to the period, so their hair-styles must be authentic. The person responsible for this area of the production is chief make-up and hair artist Aileen Seaton.

'We went through mountains of books to get the hair right for the period,' says Aileen. 'Apart from Emilia Fox, most of the female artists ended up wearing wigs which we had specially made for them. We would take the artist in and decide what was right for the character, trying, where possible, to get a range of colours.

'Diana Rigg had quite strong ideas about how Mrs Danvers should wear her hair. She didn't want the classical bun, which they always seem to put the housekeeper in and which, to be perfectly honest, looks a bit tired and old and not very interesting. Instead she opted for a dark, steel grey wig in a heavy straight bob that is reasonably undressed. A lot of people had their hair like that in those days although the usual way of doing Twenties hair is to do it quite waved and fussy. This is a much more simple approach and a nice way of doing it without going for the bun. To make the style quite functional, which is obviously something which would be important to Mrs Danvers, she has a little clip holding her hair back.

'Faye Dunaway's wig was more stylised. Mrs Van Hopper would have had more money than Mrs Danvers and so would have had a more up-to-the-minute style. Grey wasn't right for Mrs Van Hopper because she had the money to spend on getting her hair done so we chose a really striking red wig. Faye, who is naturally blonde, had never been red before but she absolutely adored it. The wig worked perfectly for her and made her feel right for the part — it gave her something to lock on to. It really suited her but, above all, it was the ideal colour for the character because whilst red is very nice, it can also be quite tacky.

Beatrice offers a sym-pathetic ear to the young bride.

'We've had a lot of fun changing people's appearances and it's a great plus if they'll go for it. I think Geraldine James would have been game to have had her hair cut short as Beatrice but for the fact that she was due to do another series of *Band of Gold* in which her hair is long. Geraldine's own hair is very blonde which wouldn't have been quite right for Beatrice but we would have been able to put some colouring on it to make it a little darker. Otherwise, apart from the length, her own hair would have been perfect. But as it was, we had to fit her with a gold-en coloured wig. I must say it worked wonderfully. It had big waves in it and made her look really young.

'The one person whose hair we were able to cut short was Emilia Fox. Her hair was much longer when she came to us but she was perfectly happy to have it cut. Indeed she preferred to have it cut the right length for the part rather than have to wear a wig. We tried a couple of wigs on her to check for the length and then decided on a length that was not too fashionable for the time, because fashion-able was very short. After all, the character she plays is not fashion-conscious and also, because she lives in the country, she would probably only have her hair cut now and then rather than keeping up with trends in a London way.

'The second Mrs de Winter is a simple girl who wouldn't normally wear much make-up. We wanted to retain aspects of the character description in the book, but for her to look prettier to the eye. We wanted to avoid the dowdy, pasty look which is fine for a little while but I'm not sure you would want to watch four hours of it. In the book, she is shy at first but she does blossom when she meets Maxim. Emilia has a good face to work on and she's not rigid in what she likes. She is happy to experiment. So for the scene on the liner bringing the newlyweds back to England where the heroine decides to visit the beauty parlour and go glamorous in an attempt to impress Maxim, we were able to make her up and curl her hair to give her an entirely different look. Of course, Maxim didn't approve — he wasn't accustomed to seeing her like that.

'Charles Dance was quite straightforward. We did go through the motions of darkening his hair but it didn't look wonderful on him. So his hair on *Rebecca* is pretty much his own colour. And Maxim is quite a straight person.

'We did have to do a bit of facial scarring on Charles for the after-fire scenes in the south of France. But we didn't do too much because we didn't want him to be grotesque. We used a bit of wax, plastic and gelatine and put a bubbly piece on his face on the day. He liked it — it was disfiguring without being hideous.

'Crowd scenes were probably our biggest nightmare. When we filmed in the south of France, we had trouble matching up the colour of the people's skins to those in the interior French scenes which we had already shot in Britain, because everyone on the Riviera is so suntanned. People were beginning to sunbathe in the Twenties so I had applied fake suntans to our actors in Britain but I was amazed how dark everyone was in France. It was difficult juggling it so that the continuity looked right.

'For the fancy dress ball, we used lots of stock wigs and tons of make-up. If someone had a really striking costume, we had to follow it through with the make-up. Keeping 120 extras looking right in the sun all day was a daunting task. No matter how many people you have looking after them, either the make-up starts to fall apart or the actors get too hot, or they lose things or try to take their lipstick off. Keeping the Twenties lipstick colours on them was quite challenging. They're not always the prettiest of colours — dark, heavy reds, maroons and bright reds — and not everyone wants to wear them. So it was a struggle getting 120 people to stay right because they do sneak off at lunchtime when they think nobody's looking and do their own make-up. Again for continuity purposes, you have to keep your eye on it.'

> 'We did have to do a bit of facial scarring on Charles for the after-fire scenes in the south of France. But we didn't do too much ...'

The fancy dress ball
at Manderley, the
highlight of the social
calendar.

CHAPTER SEVEN

The Stars of Rebecca

CHARLES DANCE
as
MAXIM DE WINTER

It is difficult to imagine someone with the composed aura of Charles Dance being reduced to a nervous wreck by a car, but that is precisely what happened on *Rebecca*.

'I'm afraid I don't have great affection for vintage cars,' he admits. 'The car we used was a 1927 Lanchester which had been lovingly restored by its owner. It was a beautiful-looking car, but hell to drive. Apart from anything else, you can't leap in

Maxim de Winter takes the young girl for a drive along the coastal road.

and out of it with any style. Just attempting a three-point turn reduced me to a puddle of sweat and I could see the owner wince every time I grated the gears. Because they don't have syncromesh gears, unless you get the revs absolutely right, the thing won't engage. It doesn't matter how hard you try – you can't crash your way in. You simply have to stop and start all over again, which doesn't make for smooth film-making, especially if you're pushed for time.

'I did quite a bit of driving as Maxim – in Hampshire, Devon and in the hills above Nice. The only time a double was brought in was for the scene where I nearly drove off the edge of a cliff. I did it up to the point that it was dangerous and then the stunt guy took over. I pretended to swerve and Emilia screamed. Mind you, she screamed a lot at my driving anyway!'

For Dance, *Rebecca* provided a happy reunion with director Jim O'Brien and co-star Geraldine James, both colleagues from *The Jewel in the Crown*. 'It was my agent who first told me about *Rebecca*. I said: "Who's directing it?" and he answered, "Jim O'Brien." So I rang Jim and he asked me whether I was interested in playing Maxim de Winter. I said: "Of course I am." To me, Maxim is one of the great romantic heroes in literature and since I haven't been offered any of the others, I was keen to do this!

'After that, it was a case of persuading everybody else involved that I was right for the part because when it's a co-production, there are bound to be

The cast and production team take a break from the mid-day sun.

different opinions. I believe some people think that Maxim should be darker but there is no mention in the book about the colour of Maxim's hair or in fact whether he's got any hair at all. For all I know, Daphne du Maurier might have seen him as bald.

'It always helps to work with people one likes and so I was pleased to be teaming up with Geraldine James again. After *The Jewel in the Crown*, we did a play called *Turning Over* and we had been talking about working together again for ages. And I think we're quite a passable brother and sister.'

Dance continues: 'Having been offered the part of Maxim, I then read the book for the first time. I did see the Hitchcock film on television about thirty-five years ago, probably on a wet Sunday afternoon, but I can't remember much about it, and I only saw something like ten minutes of the BBC adaptation. I just wasn't in the right place at the right time when it was on. And I deliberately didn't look at them before doing this.

'It is, of course, a wonderful story and a book that has been widely read. There are millions of devotees of Daphne du Maurier and of *Rebecca* but, whilst trying to please them, I also wanted to play the role for the benefit of those who hadn't read the book. It's like when you do Shakespeare, you must always approach it in the belief that there are people out there who have never seen it and are coming to the story afresh. *Rebecca* is a very difficult book to dramatise successfully but

Maxim wonders whether he has been selfish in marriage.

Arthur Hopcraft has succeeded. In my opinion, we are doing it in the right format. It is far too dense a story to be done as a single film and I don't think it can take drawing out to six parts. So two batches of two hours seems about right. It is a very passionate story – it has to be for the second Mrs de Winter to forgive Max for what she knows he's done. And the love affair between them is a very passionate one. The passion is understated in the book but I certainly don't feel we have over-stated it. I hope we have got the balance just about right. The whole thing is subjec-tive because it is seen through the heroine's eyes and I know Jim O'Brien's inten-tion was to shoot it in a very subjective way.'

For any actor, one of the great attractions about playing Maxim de Winter is the complex nature of his personality. There are so many sides to his character, which makes it difficult to evaluate whether he is an honourable man who is mere-ly a victim of circumstance, or genuinely evil. It is extremely rare for a self-con-fessed murderer to be perceived as a hero, but that is how the vast majority of readers view Maxim. Charles Dance acknowledges the dilemma.

'Maxim is an extremely complicated character to play, to make believable and to make acceptable. I don't care whether he's sympathetic or not, although I am told that Maxim and his situ-ation are irresistible to women. It's my job to present him in an uncompromising way because he's written in an uncompromis-ing way. All that one can cling on to is that his crime was a crime of passion which has always been looked upon with a degree of leniency and understanding.

> **'It is a very passionate story – it has to be for the second Mrs de Winter to forgive Max for what she knows he's done.'**

'I had to get inside the character and to see what made him do the things he did. All of us have experienced a range of emo-tions in our lives and been in a range of situations. We've all been in love at some point; we've all been unhappy; we've all been confused; we've all been exposed as liars, no matter how trivial. I've never murdered anybody, but I've definitely been in love and it is a state of being that lifts you to the heights of happiness and plunges you into the depths of despair. It is euphoric, confusing, all of those things. Out of these moods can come the most extreme actions, murder being one of them.

'Maxim's predicament can be viewed in a number of ways. One could suppose that he is a rather dry old stick, who suddenly found himself married to this bub-bly, vivacious woman, and it was just too much for him. But you have to think of it in the context of that period and that class. There were certain standards and codes of behaviour and a greater dependence on what people thought. And Maxim found himself in unfamiliar territory. I just have to accept that he is going to be under-stood, that he is going to be sympathised with and that he is going to be liked. But what intrigues me is how people who are not familiar with the book will see him.'

Charles Dance was born in Worcestershire on 10 October 1946. His mother worked in a Lyons Corner House; his father, a civil engineer, died when Charles was four. When his mother remarried, Charles was brought up on the edge of Dartmoor and educated in Plymouth where he excelled at athletics and was a schoolboy 400 metres champion. On leaving grammar school, he attended Plymouth College of Art before gaining a diploma in graphic design from Leicester College of Art. Back in Plymouth and still unsure as to which direction his career should take (his early jobs included a £2-a-week labourer and a shop window-dress-er for Burton's), his thoughts turned to acting and he took weekly lessons from two

Maxim takes his dog Jasper for a scamper in the beautiful grounds of Manderley.

retired RADA coaches at a local public house. He paid them in beer, and by digging their gardens. To put it mildly, it was an unconventional training.

He met his future wife, Joanna, when he was working as a waiter at the Sombrero Café near Plymouth College of Art and they married in 1970. Meanwhile he made his acting debut in repertory theatre at Colwyn Bay in North Wales. Television work began to accumulate from the mid-Seventies, notably in *Edward VII* (where he played the Duke of Clarence), *Father Brown* with Kenneth More, *The Professionals* and *Raffles*. He enjoyed great success with the Royal Shakespeare Company and, in 1977, he played the evil Klaus in the Bond film *The Spy Who Loved Me*, although he later said of the experience: 'We spent three weeks in Corfu and all I said was "Get in" before being bumped off with a harpoon in my back.' He also appeared in *For Your Eyes Only*, but turned down the opportunity to screen test for the role of Bond himself, a decision which he subsequently said he regretted.

He continued to appear in quality television productions such as *Little Eyolf* (as Borghehm) and *Nancy Astor* (as Edward Hartford Jones), but it was the role of Sergeant Guy Perron in *The Jewel in the Crown* which really made his name and earned him the BAFTA Award for Best Actor. Sections of the press hailed him as an overnight success, failing to recognise the fact that he had been toiling away for fifteen years.

Thereafter Charles Dance was in demand to play suave leading men of good breeding. He won a legion of female admirers although he protested: 'I'm not a matinée idol, I'm an actor.' Among his fans was the Princess of Wales but when he was introduced to her at the 1984 Cannes Film Festival, he was hit by an attack of nerves. 'When we finally spoke,' he recalls, 'I was so tongue-tied all I could say was she looked wonderful.'

The following year he starred alongside Meryl Streep in the hit movie *Plenty*. Tragically, on the day he landed the role, he learned that his mother, Eleanor, had collapsed and died on the platform at London's Victoria Station on her way home from holiday.

In 1986, he starred with Eddie Murphy in *The Golden Child* and took his family (Joanna, son Oliver and daughter Rebecca) out to Hollywood for a while. But he soon grew tired of the money-orientated lifestyle. Following a succession of TV movies – Dr Edward Forester in *First Born*, Ian Fleming in *Goldeneye* and Erik in *The Phantom of the Opera* – he was cast as the eye-changing hitman out to get Arnold Schwarzenegger in the blockbuster *Last Action Hero*. He remembers how he was accidentally sent the wrong script, so that his character's entry into the film was described with the words: "The door opens and there stands Alan Rickman." On the first day of shooting, Dance wore a T-shirt which read: "I'm cheaper than Alan Rickman."

A frank and likeable man, he remains wary of his image. 'When I did *The Big Breakfast* a couple of years ago, I heard them announce me as the debonair Charles Dance. It's something I'm determined to get rid of. I'm not debonair – I just happen to be able to play people who are debonair.'

The latest in that illustrious line is Maxim de Winter, although there was precious little that was romantic about the night shoot at Charlestown where he and the crew were left high and dry. 'That night, we certainly learned the truth of the saying: "Time and tide wait for no man!" We were completely taken by surprise. We broke for supper and by the time we came back, the boat was marooned on some rocks and the tide had gone out 50ft. We ended up doing the scene on the beach but thanks to the wonders of film-making, I could have been in the middle of the North Sea. I was like the boy standing on the burning deck!

'I didn't mind too much because the sea was very choppy that night. I'm a bit of a kid at heart so I like all that rough stuff but I must admit I was a bit apprehensive when I arrived at the location and saw how choppy it was. In the end, I was quite happy to do the scene on dry land.'

Diana Rigg as the sinister housekeeper, Mrs Danvers.

DIANA RIGG
as
MRS DANVERS

Opposite:
In Rebecca's smoke-
filled bedroom,
Maxim finds Mrs
Danvers.

With Manderley
ablaze, Maxim braves
the searing heat and
choking smoke to rush
upstairs in search of
the trapped Mrs
Danvers.

Diana Rigg's heart has always been on the stage. Over a career spanning thirty-five years, she has chosen her television appearances carefully, so it was a veritable coup to get her to star in *Rebecca*.

'The stage is the place for me,' she says, a statement supported by the fact that only a few years ago she was happy to earn £165 a week on stage in Liverpool while her hotel room cost her more than £40 a day. 'Television helps subsidise that sort of thing,' she adds.

Her television roles may have been comparatively sparse but they have been nonetheless memorable, from that Sixties icon, the leather-clad Emma Peel in *The Avengers*, through to the vengeful mother in the award-winning *Mother Love* via scene-stealing guest appearances on *Morecambe and Wise*, *Parkinson* and *The Muppets*. Hilary Heath, producer of *Rebecca*, has no doubt that, in Mrs Danvers, Diane Rigg has conjured up another superb performance.

'We talked a lot about Mrs Danvers and how Diana saw her. We came to the

*In Rebecca's smoke-
filled bedroom,
Maxim finds Mrs
Danvers.*

conclusion that Mrs Danvers had probably gone to Manderley as a maid in her twenties and had subsequently been promoted to being Rebecca's personal maid. Consequently, Rebecca became her life and Mrs Danvers was absolutely devoted to her. She lived through Rebecca and that gives some pathos to the woman – it doesn't just make Mrs Danvers evil. It makes her also very sad and when she breaks down at the end, it is a very sad moment. Her loss was probably greater that anybody's. In the scene where she is showing the heroine around Rebecca's room and is talking about her clothes, you can see how great her loss was. Diana did the breakdown absolutely beautifully – it was just heartbreaking.

Diana Rigg was born in Doncaster on 20 July 1938. At the age of seven, she was sent to boarding school in Buckinghamshire. It was not an enjoyable experience, principally because of the appalling conditions, and the young Diana was hugely relieved when her parents moved back to Leeds and sent her to Fulneck School in Pudsey. There she came under the wing of theatre-loving teacher Sylvia Greenwood who was to exert a profound influence on her life. Diana's first role was a tiny part as Goldilocks in the school play, at the age of nine, but Mrs Greenwood saw enough to realise she had unearthed a rare talent. 'She had a magnificent voice, even at that age,' said Mrs Greenwood many years later. 'You didn't have to tell her what to do on stage. She was a natural.'

> 'She lived through Rebecca and that gives some pathos to the woman – it doesn't just make Mrs Danvers evil.'

Diana's parents were not particularly interested in the theatre. She did not make her first visit until the age of twelve, and then it was to pantomime. When they finally took her to see Shakespeare's *Henry VIII* at Leeds, she was captivated and asked to go again. Diana fell in love with the theatre and Mrs Greenwood suggested she consider a career as an actress.

Overcoming her parents' anxieties, Diana went to the Royal Academy of Dramatic Art where they seemed at a loss as to what to do with her. She remembers: 'I was a tall young woman who was patently never going to be a juvenile or character actor. One teacher wrote in my report that I was not cut out for the theatre. She then worked as an enthusiastic assistant stage manager in repertory at York and Chesterfield. At the latter venue, she earned a rave review from the local paper's drama critic... even though she was only the prompter. She made her presence felt so much throughout the performance that the critic suggested she should have taken a curtain call. 'It was just enthusiasm,' she laments, 'but the cast didn't talk to me after that.'

In 1962, she joined the Royal Shakespeare Company but two years later left to star in *The Avengers*. Her place at the RSC was taken by a young actress named Glenda Jackson.

Some of Diana's classical peers viewed her decision to join a popular escapist television series with scorn. 'In those days, television was a step down,' she explains. 'But acting was my profession and I wanted to dip my toe in every part of it. I wanted to show that it was possible to do the whole range.'

As Emma Peel she became what she jokingly described as 'a pre-puberty sex symbol', receiving bundles of fan mail from schoolboys, 'mostly from the fourth form and under.' She did not always enjoy the attention which went with her newfound fame and once locked herself in the lavatory to escape from admirers at the Motor Show. Nor could she understand why she was – and indeed still is – seen as something of a sex symbol.

'The idea of me being a sex symbol has always made me laugh,' she says. 'To be a sex symbol you have to take yourself seriously. I have a very low esteem about my looks and even when I was a teenager, I dressed like a middle-aged woman. I don't take compliments very well and I suppose a lot of it goes back to my childhood. I was brought up only to glance in the mirror and if my mother caught me staring into it, she would tell me not to be so vain. She was a no-nonsense Yorkshire woman who believed that children should be seen and not heard so compliments were very thin on the ground. I must admit that I found the mass lust that surrounded me during and after *The Avengers* very hard to cope with, particularly when there was nothing about my body that I liked.'

After two years on *The Avengers* she left and returned to the theatre, with occasional breaks for film and television. 'I've never really had a career plan,' she insists. ' I've just ricocheted from one job to another.'

Throughout her life, she has always put her family first. She turned down the prestigious female lead in the 1969 movie *Paint Your Wagon* with Lee Marvin because her father was seriously ill. And when, at thirty-eight, she gave birth to daughter Rachael (by her second husband, Scottish landowner Archie Stirling), she concentrated on motherhood. 'I wanted to spend as much time as possible with Rachael. I even chose some parts for her. I did a Muppet film and the children's TV series *The Worst Witch* because I wanted her to see what I do when I go to work.'

Prior to Mrs Danvers, Andrew Davies's *Mother Love* was arguably her most sinister television role to date. 'That was one of the few times I found myself taking the part home. I had to take a long shower each day to wash her off. If you're playing someone psychotic twelve hours a day, it rubs off.'

Awarded the CBE in 1987 and made a Dame in 1994, Diana Rigg is justifiably regarded as one of our most accomplished actresses. It has been a rewarding journey from Goldilocks to Mrs Danvers.

EMILIA FOX
as the second
MRS DE WINTER

It was a day Emilia Fox will never forget. On the morning of Thursday 30 May she sat the last part of her English finals at Oxford and then dashed off to London to start rehearsals for her first major acting role, that of the second Mrs de Winter in *Rebecca*.

Opposite:
Emilia Fox as the
second Mrs de Winter.

'It was an unbelievable week,' says Emilia, known to all as 'Millie'. 'On the Wednesday, I did an exam in the morning at Oxford before rushing to London for the read-through on *Rebecca* in the afternoon. I then drove back and had to revise for my exam on the Romantics the following day. I stayed up all night on that and then went into my last exam on the Thursday. And after that I saw Oxford no more because I missed all the usual post-exam celebrations to fly off for my first rehearsal. It was all very exciting, although I was in a bit of a daze by the end of the week. Luckily, I managed to get a 2:1 in my English which was something of a relief.'

As the daughter of Edward Fox and Joanna David, it might be assumed that Millie would automatically follow in their illustrious footsteps, but she was anxious

Maxim and his bride
to be drink coffee at a
café in the hills above
Monte Carlo.

to keep her options open. 'I did a bit of acting at school. I was Mary in the school nativity play when I was five and two years later, I played a goblin king in a play about King Arthur. I had this wonderful costume with a beard and crown, all made by my mother. It was terribly exciting.

'As I got older, I thought acting might be fun to go into but I wanted to go to university first and have the opportunity to broaden my mind. My parents never tried to influence me one way or the other. They knew that if it was something I wanted to do, then fine. As soon as I got to university, I set up a company with some friends and we started doing a lot of classical plays, which is quite unusual for Oxford.' Among the parts she played there were Titania in *A Midsummer Night's Dream*, Laura in *The Glass Menagerie* and Nina in *The Seagull*. 'I was very lucky to be able to do that because I might never get to play those parts again. So university confirmed my interest in acting and allowed me to show what I could do without too much pressure of being in the public eye.'

While still at Oxford, Millie played Georgiana Darcy in the BBC's acclaimed production of *Pride and Prejudice* and then in the 1996 Easter holidays, her agent began sending her up for auditions.

'That seemed the right time to pursue parts so that I could work after my finals. I auditioned for *Rebecca* at the same time as I was revising for my mocks so there is quite a nice parallel in my life between auditions and mocks and the read-through and the finals. When I told my mother I was auditioning for Mrs de Winter, which was, of course, the same part she had played in the BBC version of *Rebecca* in the late Seventies, she was very pleased for me but I think she was probably more worried about my exams. For my part, it was great to have a distraction. You become so focused with academic work, especially in that last year, that to have this other track, this other goal, was just a lovely release.

'I was only four when my mother did the BBC version so I've only seen bits of it. I remember going down to Cornwall with her for filming and Jeremy Brett, who played Maxim, being very kind and sweet to me. But apart from watching a tiny bit before my audition, I deliberately didn't go back to it, because I wanted my portrayal to be very different, particularly in view of the connection with my mother. I want us to be judged as two actresses, not mother and daughter. For that reason, I was delighted when I learned that neither the producer nor the director of *Rebecca* knew about my family background.

'After my audition, I rang my agent on the morning of my last mock exam, but there was no news so I had to do my final mock, not knowing whether or not I'd got the part. I did the exam, got home and then in the evening my agent called me with the good news.'

Millie was no stranger to the book. 'I had read *Rebecca* as a girl and I had read it again since – it is a story which you go back to over and over. In fact, I think I must have done the book at school because in my copy I found an essay question, but I honestly don't remember studying it.

'One of the first things I did after getting the part was to map out the journey which my character takes. In many respects, we went through the same journey together. It was much the same for me walking into the read-through as it was for

Opposite:
Maxim berates his wife for venturing near the beach.

> 'I did feel very close to her. Apart from anything else, she's my age, twenty-one, and I found myself able to identify with her...'

her arriving at Manderley for the first time. We were both meeting a whole lot of new people, although happily there was no Mrs Danvers among the cast! Beforehand, I thought of all the things I needed to know, but everyone was incredibly helpful. Jim O'Brien took me through my paces but also let me find the character so that the end result is part of me as well as his input.

'I worked with Charles Dance nearly every day and he was so helpful. I learned so much from him. And it was very exciting doing scenes with Diana Rigg who is such an experienced actress and whom I also relied upon for advice. Being a virtual newcomer to television, I also had to familiarise myself with what goes on behind the camera and so the crew took me to one side and showed me the ropes.'

Millie was able to incorporate a good deal of her own emotions into playing the heroine. 'I did feel very close to her. Apart from anything else, she's my age, twenty-one, and I found myself able to identify with her, although not in every respect. For instance, I haven't got an older husband tucked away. But if I were confronted with a character like Mrs Danvers, I think I would react in the same way as the heroine did.

'I think it's her natural qualities which attract Maxim in the first place. Her youth is what Maxim can feed off and it is his age and experience which fascinates her. I wanted her to have a strength in her mind, I didn't want her to appear to be wet. She's not a feather that is battered about at first – it's simply her situation. Initially she does keep everything to herself, but with Mrs Van Hopper it's not her position to express views on anything. But deep down, she knows what she wants. She has dreams, and Maxim happens to be the answer to them.

'To my mind, the key moment in their relationship is when he confesses that he killed Rebecca. She then makes that decision to stand by him and really expresses her love for him, even before he reveals that he hated Rebecca. She had been living under this illusion that he was completely in love with Rebecca but then she is allowed into that secret, which no one else knows, and that suddenly pulls them much closer together. She had never ever lied before and whilst she doesn't exactly lie for him, she does cover up for him. That is because she is determined to keep their relationship intact at all costs. Her huge strength is her complete love for him and she has to show her backbone then to support this man who is under huge pressure.'

Everyone concerned with the production is convinced that the delightful Millie has a bright future. She herself says that filming *Rebecca* has taught her a lot. 'We worked under so many different conditions that I learned how your concentration has to be spot on, no matter how hot it is. I realise how lucky I've been to get such a wonderful part so early in my career. The only trouble is it all happened so quickly. When it was finished, there seemed a rather large hole in my life. But it really has been the most fantastic year and I can honestly say I've enjoyed every second of it – even the exams.'

Opposite:
Director Jim O'Brien,
consults with Emilia
Fox.

FAYE DUNAWAY
as
MRS VAN HOPPER

Oscar-winning actress Faye Dunaway has specialised in playing strong, forthright women – like gun-toting gangster Bonnie Parker in *Bonnie and Clyde*, fiercely ambitious television presenter Diana Christensen in *Network* and Hollywood hardcase Joan Crawford in *Mommie Dearest*. So the role of the brash, opinioned Mrs Van Hopper in *Rebecca* was right up her street, even though the actress was not familiar with the works of Daphne du Maurier.

'I'd never read the book before,' she confesses. 'Although I understand she is big almost everywhere else in the world, Daphne du Maurier really isn't that well known in the US. But once I received the script, I fell in love with the part and couldn't wait to do it. Mrs Van Hopper is such a loud, colourful character. She is a snob and a gossip although, in many ways, she is rather sad, having to pay a young girl to be her companion. Maybe she hasn't got as many friends as she thinks she has.'

It appears that another attraction for Dunaway was that the part took her back to the period in history which first launched her on the road to stardom, *Rebecca* being set just a few years before *Bonnie and Clyde*.

Faye Dunaway was raised in Tallahassee, Florida, a born battler. 'Southern women are very strong,' she says. 'They are cunning and hide their strength behind a soft, pleasing femininity. I'm a fighter – I'll go to the mat for what I believe.' Her mother was equally formidable and had to be even more so after her husband walked out on the family when Faye was thirteen. The game plan was for Faye to be a store assistant at Sears of Tallahassee but she had other ideas and began to pursue an acting career instead. She enrolled in a drama club at high school and later joined the theatre department at Boston University. In the finest tradition of Hollywood starlets, she subsidised her training by working as a cocktail waitress.

Her film career took off in 1967. After *Hurry Sundown* (an uninspired racial melodrama with Jane Fonda and Michael Caine) and the comic caper *The Happening* (with Anthony Quinn), she hit the jackpot with her third movie, starring opposite Warren Beatty in the tale of two bank robbers who terrorised America. *Bonnie and Clyde* catapulted Dunaway into the big league, but it was also a film and a character with which she could readily identify. 'I understood Bonnie – she was my soul mate. She was a frustrated southern girl who was just dying to get out. In the same way, I knew when I was sixteen if I didn't get out of Tallahassee, the place would suffocate the life out of me. So Bonnie was in my blood.'

The following year, she played an insurance investigator alongside Steve McQueen in *The Thomas Crown Affair* and succeeded in making a game of chess appear sexy. The mid-Seventies was a particularly productive period, with

> Bonnie and Clyde catapulted Dunaway into the big league, but it was also a film and a character with which she could readily identify.

Opposite:
Faye Dunaway as Mrs Van Hopper.

Chinatown and *The Towering Inferno* (both 1974) and, two years later, *Network*, the film for which she finally won an Academy Award after two unsuccessful nominations.

The morning after the Oscar ceremony, Dunaway had her picture taken with the award by British photographer Terry O'Neill. At the time, she was married to rock singer Peter Wolf of the J Geils Band, but soon she and O'Neill fell in love.

'What had begun as a flirtation between us mushroomed into a serious affair,' she says. 'We would sit for hours and talk and laugh. At the time we met, I was going through a very turbulent period. Peter wanted me to give our marriage another chance and I found myself pulled in two directions emotionally.'

Dunaway moved to Britain for ten years. She and O'Neill married in 1982 but divorced five years later whereupon she returned to Hollywood, hoping to pick up the threads of her career. It was a difficult reunion. 'I'd been away for a decade and I had people telling me it was too late for me to get back into films. They are all too anxious in Hollywood to count you out on the grounds of age, the fact that you are no longer a big box-office name, all kinds of stuff like that. With me, it was a case of out of sight, out of mind.'

A further blow came when Andrew Lloyd Webber unceremoniously dropped her from the Los Angeles production of *Sunset Boulevard*.

She has a reputation for being fiery and demanding, often caused, she maintains, because people tend to confuse her with the strident women she plays. She has certainly had one or two spats with directors in the past, notably with Roman Polanski on *Chinatown*. Infuriated when she turned up late on set, he leaned over and tugged a hair from her head. Even after the furious row which followed, she turned in a consummate performance on screen. The lady is a professional.

At fifty-five, Faye Dunaway feels more content than she has for a long time. Much of it is down to her sixteen-year-old son Liam from her marriage to Terry O'Neill. 'Motherhood changed me a lot. The early years with Liam were invaluable for me – they taught me to have more fun and really loosened me up. There was also that sense of having an enormous responsibility for another person. It made me realise there was somebody else more important than me. It certainly got rid of a lot of ego.'

Mrs Van Hopper, fuelled with champagne, mentions Rebecca to Maxim.

JONATHAN CAKE
as
JACK FAVELL

For Jonathan Cake, landing the part of Rebecca's menacing cousin Jack Favell was a gamble that paid off. In a cast full of star names, he was aware that he didn't yet come into that category despite extensive experience in the theatre and a list of television credits including *Wings, Goodnight Sweetheart* and *Frank Stubbs.* So he decided to do something to catch the attention of director Jim O'Brien, producer Hilary Heath and casting director Doreen Jones.

'I knew that *Rebecca* was a co-production and that the Americans and the Germans both wanted a big name to play Favell. When I went along for my first reading, doubts were expressed as to whether, in my early thirties, I was old enough to play him convincingly. At the time, I had a heavy growth of stubble so, before I came back for the second reading, I chose to grow a moustache and really dress up for the part. I thought the moustache would make me seem older and more caddish, like Favell ought to be.

'Unfortunately, the few days between the two readings didn't allow me to grow much of a moustache so on the morning of the second audition, I touched it up with mascara to make it look more impressive. I then put on my only suit, greased back my hair and set off. Travelling to the audition on the tube, I must have looked like a Cuban drug smuggler!

'Dressing for the part at auditions is always a gamble. You never know if the director will think your efforts are just a cheap imitation of wardrobe, in which case it can count against you. But I'm pleased to say on this occasion, it paid off and I was absolutely delighted to get the part. I did finally manage to grow a proper moustache but I couldn't wait to shave it off the moment I'd finished filming. I was fed up with being mistaken in the street for England goalkeeper David Seaman.'

Jonathan admits that he has never read the novel in its entirety or seen the Hitchcock film of *Rebecca.* 'I was desperate to see the film and to see George Sanders' portrayal of Favell. It was actually on re-release in London at the time but I never got round to seeing it. Perhaps it wasn't such a bad thing because a lot of people had warned me against going – they said Sanders' performance would have influenced me too much. Then on the first day of rehearsals, Tom Chadbon, who plays Crawley, remarked: "You've seen the film then!" He thought my reading contained distinct flavours of Sanders. But it was obviously a case of us both taking a similar approach. In fact, I'm much younger than Sanders was when he made the film and I think in the end, my age counted in my favour because they wanted someone of a different generation to Charles Dance.

'Favell is a fabulously vivid character, very ripe and fruity, and I love the way the adaptation brings out the dangerous, violent and ugly passions in the story. It was great to play a baddie although I'm not sure that he was as wicked as

'...it must be said that no matter how noble his sentiments, he doesn't express them particularly well. Blackmail wasn't one of his cleverer moves.'

Opposite:
Jonathan Cake as
Jack Favell.

Jack Favell does not believe that Rebecca committed suicide.

Daphne du Maurier painted him. She was amazingly condemnatory. As an actor, you have to find out what motivates your character to behave in the way he does. Favell is motivated by a sense of injustice and this comes across in his feelings of anger and passion. I tried to see him as essentially a decent man, and to look for the sympathetic side to his character, although it must be said that no matter how noble his sentiments, he doesn't express them particularly well. Blackmail wasn't one of his cleverer moves.

'He is a very important character. Let's face it, the story wouldn't have its last hour had not Favell been so devoted to Rebecca that he becomes intent on proving that it was Maxim who had killed her. And this quest for justice spills over into class resentment. Favell is a socialist – in as much as he is keen on sharing other people's wives – and is appalled when the ruling classes take Maxim's side. It's like the old boy network. Favell feels that there has been a gross miscarriage of justice. He feels like an outsider who is kept out by the combination of power and money. He has this sneering resentment. He is treated badly, so he behaves badly. When it came to the scene in the library with the heroine, I tried to play it as sincerely as

possible. Favell tries to convince her that it's not him who is the big bad wolf – he's just an ordinary chap. She feels threatened by him but he's not the murderer. The person she should be scared of is her husband.'

Jonathan revelled in creating the right look for Favell although he does concede: 'It's what you say that is important, not how you look. But Favell clearly takes a pride in his appearance – he does see himself as a ladies' man. I wore this dogtooth check suit which looked appropriately rakish.

'It was funny because the job I'd done immediately before *Rebecca* was another period piece, the BBC's adaptation of Anne Brontë's *The Tenant of Wildfell Hall*. In that, I played Ralph and wore a ring with a large R on it. Lo and behold, on my first day on *Rebecca*, I was presented with the same ring, this time to denote Favell's love for Rebecca. So I had returned the ring one week and got it back the next! The two productions obviously used the same costumier.'

Favell's other prop was a cigarette. 'Smoking was a sign of decadence in those days so a cigarette was an ideal prop for him. I actually had to learn to smoke for the part, because it was something I had never done before, nor had any wish to do.

Maxim punches Jack Favell who has just accused him of murdering Rebecca.

Sadly, after getting through packet after packet in endless takes, I became hooked on them. Each morning, I yearned for that first rush of nicotine...

'Another thing I had to get used to was driving. I did pass my test about five years ago, purely as a qualification on my CV, but I've hardly driven since. It's just not something I want to do around London. But Favell had this 1926 custard-coloured Vauxhall two-seater which I had to drive for a few scenes. And there was I, an extremely shaky driver, sitting in this splendid old car which the Vauxhall people took great delight in telling me was worth £150,000. I don't mind admitting I was glad to get it over with and get the car back in one piece.'

Jonathan was born in the genteel south coast resort of Worthing. Although there is no theatrical background in his family (his father ran his own business and his mother works at a sixth-form college), he showed signs of acting ability from an early age. 'I've acted since I was eight,' he says. 'I was one of those kids with too much energy and I channelled that into performing. I won acting cups all along the south coast and then at fourteen, I joined the National Youth Theatre, playing Falstaff in *Henry IV, Part One*, Brutus in *Julius Caesar* and Azdak in *The Caucasian Chalk Circle*.'

At Cambridge University he excelled at sports and earned his Rugby Blue. He graduated in English but was still not sure which path his career would take. 'I wanted something other than acting to claim me but at the end of my degree course, I had to acknowledge that there was nothing else I was trained to do.' So he joined the Bristol Old Vic Theatre School where he played such diverse roles as God in *The Mysteries* and Harry the Horse in *Guys and Dolls*. He went on to enjoy a stint at the Royal Shakespeare Company and to establish a reputation as one of the country's most promising young actors, both on stage and in television.

The start of 1996 saw him working with Bill Nighy on *True Blue*, the film of the 1987 Oxford Boat Race mutiny. 'It's the story of how the Oxford crew mutinied about the American-style training techniques that had been introduced into their preparation for the race. I'd barely been in a boat before in my life so I had to learn to row. We had four weeks of intensive training followed by eight weeks' filming, much of it on the Thames. It was tremendous fun to do although I would go to the river each morning, dreading that I would mess it up. And as the stroke, if I messed it up, I'd mess everyone else up too. As an ex-Cambridge man, the one thing that was somewhat disconcerting was wearing the embossed vest of Oxford. I know you tend to think that the rivalry between the two camps is pretty friendly, but the truth of the matter is that when you're at Cambridge, there really is an inbuilt hatred towards Oxford. So pretending to row for them was a strange experience.'

After finishing adaptations of Brontë and du Maurier, Jonathan's next job took him off on a characteristically unusual tangent – playing Rex the Lothario cow in comedian Eddie Izzard's *Cows* for Channel 4. 'It's typical Eddie Izzard – very bizarre and very funny. It is set in a world of bovine emancipation where all the cows rise up on two hooves and make a stand. They adopt human personalities and consequently display all the human weaknesses. I had to spend 15 hours a day in this huge padded cow suit, complete with latex head. It made me look the size of a small leisure centre. It was pretty uncomfortable. I lost quite a bit of weight and had to take salt tablets.'

All in all, Jonathan Cake has learned a lot of new skills over the past year. So if there's a part for a cow which drives a car, chain-smokes and likes to go rowing on the river, he's your man.

GERALDINE JAMES
as
BEATRICE

The make-up department prepare Geraldine James (Beatrice) for the grand fancy dress ball.

The last time Geraldine James appeared with Charles Dance on television, the pair were locked in a passionate love scene which reduced her to fits of giggles.

It was on *The Jewel in the Crown* where Geraldine played Sarah Layton, the

member of a typical Raj military family, who fell for Dance's Guy Perron. 'I could hardly stop laughing during our love scenes,' she admits. 'It wasn't Charles – just the absurdity of the situation. When the director is yelling things like "put a bit more passion into it" and "come on, Charlie, get your leg up", it's pretty difficult to keep a straight face! Fortunately, that was one of the last scenes shot and by then Charles and I knew each other well enough to be able to laugh about it.

'I had been wanting to work with Charles again for some time so when Jim O'Brien, who also worked on *The Jewel in the Crown*, sent me the script for *Rebecca* and asked me to play Maxim's sister Beatrice, I was delighted to accept.'

Jim O'Brien confirms: 'I wanted Geraldine as Beatrice and was thrilled when she said yes. Beatrice is Maxim's slightly outrageous sister, a character who could be played as a complete fool. But Geraldine makes her credible and ensures that she is not just a tweedy country stereotype.'

Geraldine James was raised in Berkshire, the daughter of an eminent cardiologist, and caught the acting bug at an all-girl boarding school, Down House, near Newbury. 'I was not very good at games or academic subjects and although I played the piano and clarinet, I was not terribly good. What I did excel at was being naughty. I was very good at being sent out of class for being funny – I was the clown of the school.

'When I was eleven, I was cast in a school play as the Artful Dodger, with a collapsible top hat. I brought the house down with silly antics and it was sheer joy. I really thought I would be a comedian because I so wanted to make people laugh. From then on, the school pushed me into acting and I stayed on to do A-Levels just so that I could play Malvolio in the school production of *Twelfth Night*.

'I took it for granted that I was going to be an actress. And then I got this terrible reaction from my family. My father, particularly, wanted me to be a teacher or a doctor. It took a long time to bring him round to my way of thinking.'

After training at the Drama Centre in London, she did three years in repertory playing old ladies, young girls and wicked witches in pantomime. Her first TV role was as a croupier in an episode of *The Sweeney*, but this was quickly surpassed by that of Sandra X, the deaf and dumb prostitute in the 1977 drama-documentary *Dummy*. Although her 'lines' were only a few grunts and groans, her powerful performance earned widespread acclaim and led to roles in such TV productions as *I Remember Nelson*, *The History Man*, *Blott on the Landscape*, *Kavanagh QC* and, most recently, back on the streets as Yorkshire prostitute Rose in the hit ITV series *Band of Gold*. She also appeared in the film *Gandhi* and starred opposite Dustin Hoffman in *The Merchant of Venice*, both in the West End and on Broadway.

For a while, Hollywood beckoned, but Geraldine was more concerned with settling daughter Eleanor in at school. 'Being a mother and an actress is a tough combination. You can condition a child if you go to an office from nine to five, but acting is irregular and requires emotional commitment. I usually play screwed-up spinsters, which is difficult if you have an angelic little person waiting for you to take her for a walk. Colleagues are appalled at the parts I've turned down...'

Married to film director Joe Blatchley, Geraldine is quite happy that, at forty-six, she is still not considered a star. 'I'm just an actress,' she says. 'I'd hate to be a star – it would be too intrusive – and I do like meeting people. Whenever I've been on anything on television, people come up to me afterwards and say: "Haven't we met before?" I'm not famous enough for them to remember my name, but they know my face and think I work in the paper shop. It makes me feel a complete pillock to say: "You probably saw me on television."'

At 5ft 8in and with her strong jaw, Geraldine appears extremely capable but, she insists, looks can be deceptive. 'If I get a puncture, no one stops to help. They think: "She looks as if she can change a wheel." It's ghastly. I'd like to be soft and fluffy like Marilyn Monroe.'

LUCY COHU

as

REBECCA

When author Susan Hill brought out her sequel to *Rebecca*, actress Lucy Cohu did a photographic shoot for a magazine to tie in with publication of the book.

She recalls: 'They wanted an actress to come down and wear clothes from the twenties and to use the photos next to excerpts from Susan Hill's book. After the shoot, the magazine interviewed me. They asked: "If they ever re-make *Rebecca*, I bet you'd love to play the second Mrs de Winter?" I said: "No, no! Give me Rebecca!" It was just a throwaway line but two years later, I found myself doing just that.'

Lucy remembers first reading the book as a thirteen-year-old at Stamford High School in Lincolnshire. 'A teacher gave it to me to read and I became so hooked that I used to skip lessons in order to sneak off and read it in a quiet room. I just thought it was brilliant. After that I moved on to *Frenchman's Creek*, but *Rebecca* was always the one for me.'

As her acting career took off (last year at Birmingham, she was one of the youngest ever Lady Macbeths), Lucy was asked to audition for Rebecca. 'My agent had told me that Rebecca wouldn't be shown in full but when I met director Jim O'Brien, I was really impressed. I liked the way he talked about her and how it was obviously so important to the success of the production to get the role of Rebecca right.

'Rebecca belonged to a time when women were women, and women were wicked. She's larger than life, in the great tradition of Bette Davis and Joan Crawford. But I don't think anyone could match up to the description of her in the book, so I think it's right that she's never shown full on. By just catching glimpses of her, it retains that mystique. Otherwise, I think there would always be a disappointment because most people have read the book and therefore have an idea of how Rebecca should look.

> 'But I don't think anyone could match up to the description of her in the book, so I think it's right that she's never shown full on.'

'The book allows you to conjure up the strength of this woman. There's a passage where the second Mrs de Winter opens a book and finds a note in bold handwriting: "To Max with love." And it's signed with a brash, confident R. It's impossible to get your head round such a character – a little girl who breaks in a stallion which kicks her until she tames it, someone who has total contempt for men. She is absolutely fearless. She was born with brains, beauty and money and had nothing against her, apart from a very messed-up childhood.

'It's been lovely to do, but quite strange being filmed first through your eyes, then with the camera moving on to your mouth and your hands. Because the close-ups of her are so tight, you become far more self-conscious than if you were just playing the scene as a whole.

'I recently played another wicked woman in the Screen Two film *Loving*. It was set in the Forties and while my character's husband was away fighting the war,

I was carrying on with a chap across the road. I definitely like playing wicked women – I'm good at them – and they don't come much more wicked than Rebecca. What I'd really love is for someone to write a script about Rebecca's life. That would be fun.'

Cast List

MAXIM DE WINTER	Charles Dance
MRS DANVERS	Diana Rigg
MRS DE WINTER	Emilia Fox
MRS VAN HOPPER	Faye Dunaway
JACK FAVELL	Jonathan Cake
FRANK CRAWLEY	Tom Chadbon
BEATRICE	Geraldine James
GILES	Denis Lill
GRANNY DE WINTER	Jean Anderson
COLONEL JULYAN	Anthony Bate
DR BAKER	Timothy West
REBECCA	Lucy Cohu
FRITH	John Horsley
ROBERT	Jonathan Stokes
BEN	John Branwell
TABB	Robin Soans
CORONER	Ian McDiarmid
HARBOURMASTER	Patrick Romer
OLDEST GARDENER	Frank Doherty
HAIRDRESSER	Carla Mendonca
NURSE	Wendy Macadam
CLARICE	Kelly Reilly
NELSON	David Webb
TUDOR LADY	Zulema Dene
NAPOLEON	Michael Wynne

Production Team

EXECUTIVE PRODUCERS	Jonathan Powell
	Tim Buxton
PRODUCER	Hilary Heath
CO-PRODUCER	Andrew Warren
DIRECTOR	Jim O'Brien
EXECUTIVE PRODUCER FOR WGBH	Rebecca Eaton
EXECUTIVE PRODUCER FOR TELE-MÜNCHEN	Rikolt Von Gagern
ASSOCIATE PRODUCERS	Steve Matthews
	George Adams
SCREENPLAY BY	Arthur Hopcraft
DIRECTOR OF PHOTOGRAPHY	Rex Maidment B.S.C.
PRODUCTION DESIGNER	Caroline Amies
EDITOR	Michael Parker
SOUND RECORDIST	Peter Sutton
COSTUME DESIGNER	Elizabeth Waller
SCRIPT EDITOR	Steve Matthews
CASTING DIRECTOR	Doreen Jones
MUSIC COMPOSED BY	Christopher Gunning
CONSULTANT FOR THE DU MAURIER ESTATE	Robin Lowe
PRODUCTION MANAGER – FRANCE	Frederic Bovis
1ST ASSISTANT DIRECTOR	Nick Heckstall-Smith

2ND ASSISTANT DIRECTOR	Jamie Christopher
3RD ASSISTANT DIRECTOR	Zerlina Hughes
PRODUCTION CO-ORDINATOR	Nathalie Tanner
LOCATION MANAGER	Mark Mostyn
UNIT MANAGER	John Bamford
PRODUCTION RUNNER	Rick Barker
FLOOR RUNNER	Daniel Heath
STUNT CO-ORDINATOR	Nick Powell
SCRIPT SUPERVISOR	Sheila Wilson
FT2 CONTINUITY TRAINEE	Victoria Pike
NURSE	Patricia Barr
CAMERA OPERATOR/ STEADICAM	Peter Robertson
FOCUS PULLER	Keith Broome
CLAPPER LOADER	Mark Maidment
GRIP	Jim Monks
CAMERA TRAINEE	Stuart Chapman
STILLS PHOTOGRAPHER	Sophie Baker
SOUND RECORDIST	Peter Sutton
SOUND MAINTENANCE ENGINEER	Keith Pamplin
PRODUCTION ACCOUNTANT	Martin Cook
ASSISTANT ACCOUNTANT	Richard Wood
ART DIRECTOR	Frank Walsh
ASSISTANT ART DIRECTOR	Paul Kirby
PRODUCTION BUYER	Roger Hulme
SET DRESSER	Claire Grainger
ART DEPT JUNIOR	Edward Cotton
ASSISTANT EDITOR	Riaz Meer
SOUND EDITOR	Danny Longhurst
DUBBING MIXER	Mike Narduzzo
TRAINEE	Marian Vossaugh

CHIEF MAKE-UP & HAIR	Aileen Seaton
MAKE-UP/HAIR ARTIST	Jane Walker
WARDROBE SUPERVISOR	Colin Lavers
WARDROBE ASSISTANT	Anna Houghton
PROPERTY MASTER	Alan Bailey
C/H STAND-BY PROP	Dave Fisher
STAND-BY PROP	William Edwards
DRESSING PROP	Danny Evans
DRESSING PROP	Brian Humphrey
PROP STOREMAN	George Malin
CONSTRUCTION MANAGER	Alan Chesters
STAND-BY CARPENTER	Peter Beasley
STAND-BY RIGGER	Tom Lowen
STAND-BY STAGEHAND	David Gruar
STAND-BY PAINTER	Anthony Caccavale
GAFFER	Joe Ryan
BEST BOY	Iwan Williams
ELECTRICIAN	Terry McGuiness
ELECTRICIAN	Liam McGill
STUNT DOUBLES	Joss Gower
	Sy Hollands
DOG TRAINER	Rona Brown
VEHICLES PROVIDED BY	H. R. H. Prince Rainier of Monaco
	The Vauxhall Historic Vehicle Collection

BIBLIOGRAPHY

Cook, Judith, *Daphne*, (Bantam Press, 1991).

Forster, Margaret, *Daphne du Maurier*, (Chatto & Windus, 1993).

Shallcross, Martyn, *The Private World of Daphne du Maurier*, (Robson Books, 1991).